Glenn's
AUSTIN,
AUSTIN-HEALEY and
SPRITE
Repair and Tune-up
Guide

HAROLD T. GLENN

Member, Society of Automotive Engineers; Formerly, Instructor in Long Beach City Schools, Long Beach, Calif.

Author of Glenn's New Auto Repair Manual (Annual), Automobile Engine Rebuilding & Maintenance, Automobile Power Accessories, Exploring Automechanics, Exploring Power Mechanics, Youth at the Wheel, Automechanics, Safe Living, Foreign Car Repair Manual, and selected foreign car repair guides

ILLUSTRATED

CHILTON BOOK COMPANY
Philadelphia   New York   London

Acknowledgments

The author wishes to thank The British Motor Cor-
poration / Hambro Inc. for their assistance in furnishing
technical information and illustrations and *Road & Track*
magazine for permission to use their road test data. The
author also wishes to express special thanks to his wife,
ANNA GLENN, for her devoted assistance in proofreading
and revising the text.

HAROLD T. GLENN

In many sections the reader will note step-by-step illustrated instructions. These picture series can be identified
by a circled number in the lower right-hand corner of
each illustration. The numbers agree with the numbered
instructions in the text, and are so correlated that no legends
are required.

Contents

1
Troubleshooting

Troubleshooting is done before a unit is disassembled so that the mechanic can give the car owner an estimate of the cost of the repair job. It helps the mechanic to pinpoint the trouble so that he will know what to look for as the unit is being disassembled. Then, too, troubleshooting will frequently cut down on the amount of time spent on repair, provided that the defective section can be pinpointed accurately.

BASIC STARTING TROUBLE TESTS

When an engine is difficult to start, or does not start at all, it is necessary to use a logical procedure to locate the trouble. Basically, the problem of hard starting can be broken down into four areas of trouble: cranking, ignition, fuel, and compression. The tests are made in that order, as shown on the roadmap.

When the trouble is localized to one of these four areas, the mechanic can then proceed to make one of the more detailed tests described for each area in order to locate the exact source of trouble.

THE CRANKING SYSTEM (TEST 1)

Turn on the ignition switch and energize the starting motor. If the starting motor cranks the engine at a normal rate of speed, it is an indication that the battery, cables, starting switch, and starting motor are in good shape. A defective cranking system is evidenced by failure of the cranking motor to spin the engine at a normal rate of speed.

If the cranking system is operating satisfactorily, go on to the second test, the ignition system. If it is not operating properly, proceed to the more Detailed Tests of the cranking system which follow this section in order to isolate the trouble.

THE IGNITION SYSTEM (TEST 2)

Disconnect one spark plug wire and hold it about ¼″ (12 mm.) from the plug terminal while cranking the engine with the ignition switch turned on. A good, constantly occurring spark to the plug means that the ignition system is in good shape. No spark, a weak spark, or an irregularly occurring one means ignition trouble.

If the ignition system is operating satisfactorily, go on to the third test, the fuel system. If it is not operating properly, proceed to the more Detailed Tests of the ignition system which follow this section in order to isolate the trouble.

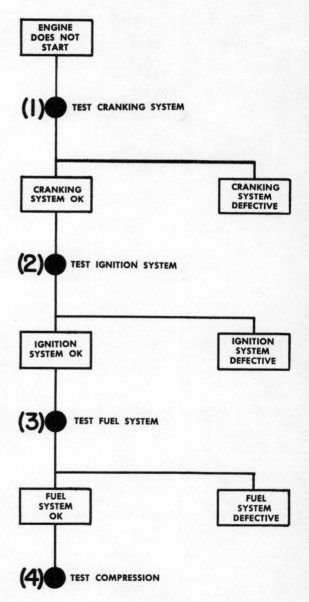

Roadmap for emergency troubleshooting when an engine does not start. The four numbered tests are referred to in the text.

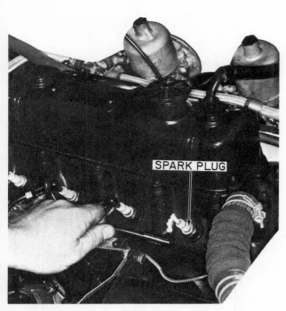

Testing the ignition system for a spark to the spark plug terminal.

THE FUEL SYSTEM (TEST 3)

Remove the air cleaner to uncover the carburetor throat. Then open and close the throttle several times. A stream of fuel will be discharged from the accelerating jet if the fuel system is in good shape. No discharge indicates that there is no fuel in the carburetor, which means trouble in the fuel system. In rare instances, the carburetor accelerating system may be defective and no fuel will be discharged even though the carburetor is full of gasoline. Usually there is a decided resistance to movement of the throttle when such a condition exists. On some carburetors, there is no acceleration pump; in this case, it is necessary to remove the float bowl cover to see whether fuel is present.

If the fuel system is operating satisfactorily, go on to the fourth test, compression. If it is not operating properly, proceed to the more Detailed Tests of the fuel system to isolate the trouble.

COMPRESSION (TEST 4)

Compression can be checked by removing a spark plug and holding a thumb over the spark plug hole while the engine is being cranked. Good compression produces a distinct pressure under your thumb as the piston rises to the top of its stroke.

Failure of an engine to start due to compression trouble is rarely encountered in the field. Most frequently, compression trouble will show up as defects in but one or two cylinders. No compression in all cylinders of an engine may occur from improper mating of the timing gears when the engine is rebuilt. It can happen on the road through jumping of a loose timing chain or the snapping of a camshaft—but this is so infrequently the case

that it can almost be ruled out as a condition causing starting trouble.

DETAILED STARTING TROUBLE TESTS

The more detailed tests which follow are to isolate the starting trouble in the defective system located by the first series of tests. Each of the four general areas of trouble is broken down further to tests of individual components. In this manner, the exact part causing the trouble can be located and replaced.

CRANKING SYSTEM

The cranking system consists of a battery, cables, starting switch, and the starting motor. Failure of the starting motor to spin the engine, or turning it too slowly, is an indication of a defect in one of the above parts.

Battery (Test 1). The battery supplies electric current for the starting motor, lights, ignition, and other electrical accessories. If the starting motor spins the engine at a fairly good rate of speed and then rapidly slows down, the battery is discharged. Turn on the lights while cranking the engine. If the lights go out, the battery is discharged. There is not enough current in a partially charged battery to supply both the starting motor and the lighting system.

A 6-volt battery with a defective cell (shorted separator) usually will not turn the starting motor at all, although it may do so for a very short period if the battery has been charged by a recent run of the engine. If such a battery is allowed to

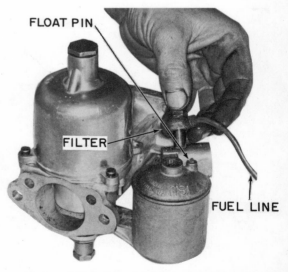

Because S.U. carburetors have no accelerator pump, it is necessary to remove the cover to see if fuel is present in the bowl. The float pin can be depressed with the ignition switch turned on to see if the electric fuel pump is operating.

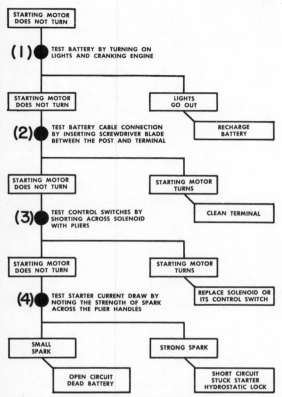

Testing a cable connection by inserting a screwdriver blade between the battery terminal and the cable connector (Test 2). If the terminal is corroded, the screwdriver blade will make contact between the two parts of the connection and the cranking motor will operate.

Roadmap for emergency troubleshooting of the cranking system when the starting motor does not turn. The four numbered tests are referred to in the text.

stand for a short time, it will lose this surface charge. A 12-volt battery may operate the starting motor with a defective cell, but it will not spin the starting motor fast enough, and starting troubles will result.

Battery Cables (Test 2). Quite frequently, a bad connection between the battery post and the battery cable will show up as a dead battery. To check this condition, insert a screwdriver blade between the battery post and the cable while having an assistant operate the starting motor switch. Try the blade on each terminal connection. Now, if the starting motor turns, evidently the connection is bad. It should be cleaned by removing the cable terminal and scraping it and the battery post until clean metal appears. Then replace and tighten the terminal securely.

Switches (Test 3). A defective switch in the starting circuit can be checked by bridging each switch in turn with a jumper wire or a pair of plier handles. Bridging the solenoid switch by-passes all other control switches and should energize the starting motor regardless of any other defect in the starting motor control circuit. Use a heavy piece of wire for this test as a thin one will become very hot

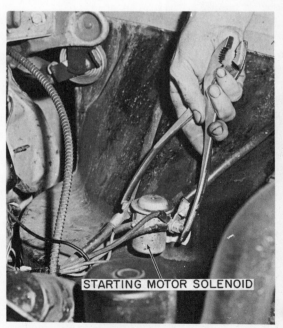

Bridging the solenoid switch (Test 3) should cause the starting motor to operate unless the trouble is in the starting motor itself.

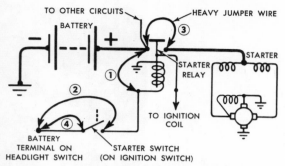

Use a jumper wire to bridge each switch in turn to find an open circuit in the starting motor control system.

from the large amount of current drawn through this circuit. Holding a hot wire may cause a serious hand injury.

If the starting motor does not operate with the solenoid switch shorted, and a fully charged battery, then the trouble must be in the starting motor itself.

Starting Motor (Test 4). The size of the spark across the plier handles in the previous test is an indication of the kind of trouble to be expected. If there is a heavy spark across the handles of the pliers, and the starting motor does not turn, it is possible that the starting motor is stuck to the flywheel, the starting motor has a short circuit, or there is a hydrostatic lock in the engine.

If there is little or no spark across the plier handles as they are moved across the solenoid switch terminals, there is an open circuit present with little or no electricity flowing. This condition can be caused by a dead battery, a poor battery terminal connection, or poor connections at the starting motor brushes due to a burned commutator or one with oil on it. If the starting motor spins, but does not crank the engine, the starting motor drive is defective.

IGNITION SYSTEM

The ignition system furnishes the electric spark which fires the mixture. Absence of a spark, or a weak spark, will cause starting trouble. Ignition troubles should be isolated by logical testing. For this purpose, the system is broken down into its smaller circuits: primary and secondary. Each of these should be broken down further and individual components tested separately.

To Test the Entire Ignition System. Remove one spark plug wire and hold it about ½" (12 mm.) away from the base of the spark plug or any metallic part of the engine. Crank the engine with the ignition switch turned on. A good spark from the wire to the metal means that the entire ignition system is in good working order. No spark, or a weak, irregularly occurring spark, means ignition

trouble which must be traced by means of the following tests:

To Test the Primary Circuit (Test 1). Loosen the distributor cap retaining bails and move the cap to one side. Remove the rotor. Turn the engine over by means of the fan belt or starting motor until the contact points close. Turn on the ignition switch. Remove the high tension wire leading to the center of the distributor cap; this is the main wire from the ignition coil which supplies the high voltage to the rotor for distribution to the spark plugs. Hold this wire about ½" (12 mm.) from any metallic part of the engine. Open and close the contact points with a screwdriver. Hold the screwdriver against the movable point only as shown. A good, regularly occurring spark from the high tension wire to ground means a good primary circuit and a good ignition coil. No spark, or a weak erratic one, from the high tension wire to ground means primary circuit trouble or a bad ignition coil.

To Test the Ignition Contact Points (Test 2). To test the condition of the ignition contact set, turn the engine over with the fan belt or starting motor until the contact points are separated. Slide

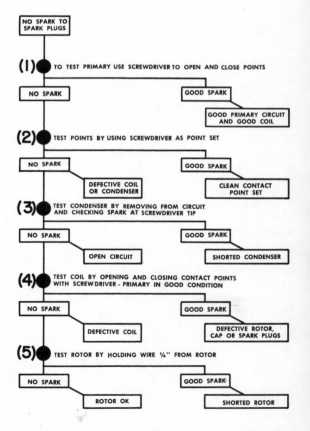

Roadmap for emergency troubleshooting of the ignition system. The five numbered tests are referred to in the text.

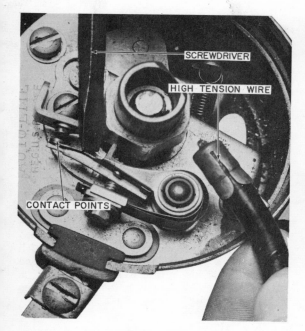

Opening and closing the ignition points with a screwdriver (Test 1), while holding the main high tension wire close to a metallic part of the engine, is a simple test of the primary circuit efficiency.

Using the screwdriver as a set of points (Test 2). Use a cleaned insulator (arrow) to keep the points apart, and then slide the screwdriver blade up and down to make intermittent contact with the point plate.

the screwdriver blade up and down, making contact between the movable point and the bottom plate of the distributor, as shown. You are now using the screwdriver tip and the bottom plate of the distributor as a set of contact points. A good spark from the high tension wire to the ground, after having had no spark in Test 1, means that you have a defective set of contact points. No spark, or a weak one, means primary circuit trouble, other than the ignition contact points, or a bad ignition coil.

To Test the Condenser (Test 3). A shorted condenser can be checked by noting, in the previous ignition contact point test (Test 2), whether or not the tip of the screwdriver blade sparked against the ground plate as it was slid up and down. No spark at the tip of the blade means either a shorted condenser or a break in the primary circuit.

This can be checked further by disconnecting the condenser case where it is screwed to the distributor (do not disconnect the condenser wire lead). Hold the condenser so that its case does not make contact with any metallic part of the distributor. Repeat the test of moving the screwdriver blade up and down while holding it against the movable point. Be sure that the contact points are open while making this test. A spark at the screwdriver tip now, which was not present with the condenser in the circuit, means that the condenser is shorted out.

No spark at the screwdriver tip with the con-

A sample of good ignition contact points (top), and a bad set (bottom) for comparison. A light gray contact surface is indicative of a set of contact points working at high efficiency. The lower set is burned black from either high voltage or oil.

A broken primary lead may not show up until you pull on it. The insulation hides the damage.

tension wire from the coil to the distributor (especially where it runs through metal conduit). A good spark here (with no spark to the spark plugs) means that the trouble must be in the distributor cap, rotor, or spark plugs. It is seldom that spark plug high tension wires (unless obviously rotted) will keep an engine from starting. To check the main high tension wire, from the coil to the center of the distributor cap, replace it with a new piece of high tension wire, or remove the old wire from the metal conduit and repeat Test 4 while keeping the suspected wire away from any grounded surface.

To Test the Distributor Rotor (Test 5). Test the distributor rotor by replacing it on the distributor shaft and holding the main high tension wire (from the coil) about ¼" (6 mm.) from the top of the rotor. With the ignition switch turned on, crank the engine with the starter. If the high tension spark jumps to the rotor, it is grounded (defective); if not, the cap must be defective. Inspect the cap for carbon tracks which indicate the passing of high voltage electricity.

FUEL SYSTEM

The purpose of the fuel system is to bring a combustible mixture of gasoline and air into the cylinders. The fuel system consists of the fuel tank, the fuel pump, and the carburetor. Troubles in the fuel system can be caused by too little fuel in the combustion chambers—or too much.

denser out of the circuit means that there is an open circuit somewhere in the primary. Check the small wire lead from the primary terminal to the movable contact point. This wire lead sometimes parts under the constant flexing of operation.

To Test the Secondary Circuit (Test 4). The secondary circuit cannot be tested until the primary circuit is functioning perfectly. If the primary circuit tests good, or after the necessary repairs have been made to the primary circuit, then the secondary circuit can be tested.

To test the secondary circuit, turn the engine over until the contact points close. Then turn on the ignition switch. Hold the main high tension wire (from the center terminal of the distributor cap) about ½" (12 mm.) from any metallic part of the engine. Open and close the contact points with a screwdriver blade held against the movable contact point only. No spark, or a weak one, from the wire to the block (*with a good primary circuit*), means a bad ignition coil or a defective main high

CARBON TRACKS

A cracked distributor cap always shows these characteristic carbon tracks. A crack between two terminals will cause misfiring, but a crack from the center terminal to the outside will prevent the engine from starting. Cracks often start from moisture on the surface of the insulating material.

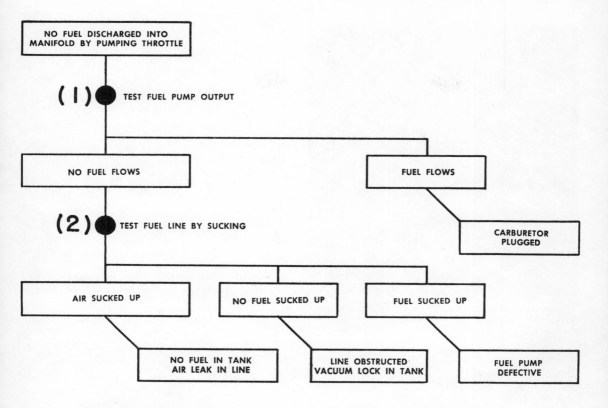

Roadmap for emergency troubleshooting of the fuel system. The two numbered tests are referred to in the text.

Too Little Fuel: TESTING THE FUEL PUMP OUTPUT (TEST 1). Disconnect the fuel line leading into the carburetor bowl and hold a container under the line to catch the gasoline as it spurts from the open end. (The ignition switch should be off; otherwise, the high tension wire should be removed from the center of the distributor cap to prevent the possibility of the engine starting and spraying gasoline all over the engine compartment.) If a good size stream of fuel flows from the pipe, and the trouble has been isolated to the fuel system, the defect must be in the carburetor. If no fuel flows, the trouble must be in the pump, lines, or gas tank.

Some European-built cars have an electric fuel pump, in which case it is necessary only to disconnect the fuel line and turn on the ignition switch for testing purposes.

It is seldom that the carburetor itself causes starting trouble. Instances have been found of an inlet strainer plugged, or the float valve needle stuck in the closed position, but these are exceptions. Cases of an automatic choke not functioning are encountered more frequently in starting trouble. If the automatic choke does not close on a cold engine being cranked, hold your hand over the top of the carburetor bore to restrict the flow

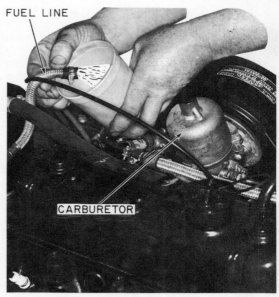

Testing the fuel pump output (Test 1). Because most models have an electric fuel pump, it is necessary only to turn on the ignition switch to start the pump in operation. On the few models with a mechanical fuel pump, cranking the engine should produce a full-sized stream of fuel each time the pump pulses.

Some fuel pumps have levers to prime the carburetor in the event that you run out of fuel. The lever can also be used to test the fuel pump.

of air, which will assist in starting the engine. Where the choke sticks in the closed position, it can be opened with your fingers and held open until the engine is firing properly.

To Test the Gas Tank and Lines (Test 2). To check the gas tank and lines, the fuel line should be disconnected at the inlet side of the fuel pump and sucked on to check for obstructions. Sucking on this line should bring up a mouthful of liquid fuel if there are no defects in the line or tank. Be sure to empty your mouth immediately and wash it out with water, if possible. If liquid fuel can be sucked up, and there is no flow out of the fuel pump, then the fuel pump is defective and must be repaired or replaced.

If only air is obtained by sucking on the line, then there is no fuel in the tank or there is an air leak in the line, probably at the flexible line leading into the fuel pump. If sucking on the line feels solid, and no fuel can be drawn up, the trouble is due to an obstruction in the line or a plugged gas tank vent.

Too Much Fuel. Too much fuel can be caused by overchoking, a defective float, or a defective needle and seat in the carburetor allowing fuel to by-pass the needle and overflow into the intake manifold. This can be seen as a steady stream of raw gasoline coming out of the main jet when the engine is being cranked. Raw gasoline may also enter the intake manifold in excessive amounts when the engine is stopped after a very hard and prolonged pull. In this case, the heat developed by the engine may cause the fuel to boil within the float chamber of the carburetor and percolate over the top of the main delivery tube into the intake

manifold. Some carburetors are vented to prevent this possibility, but there are times when this vent is not functioning properly. Excessive amounts of raw gasoline can be seen by opening the throttle fully and looking down into the intake manifold through the carburetor bore.

Sometimes black smoke coming from the exhaust pipe while the engine is being started is another sign of too much fuel. The best test, however, is the removal of a spark plug. An overchoked engine will have spark plugs wet with raw gasoline while a normal engine will have dry spark plugs.

To start an engine which has been overloaded with fuel, it is necessary first to remedy the condition causing the trouble, and then the engine can be started by opening the throttle fully, which opens the choke. Under no circumstances should the throttle be pumped, as this will force additional quantities of raw fuel into the intake manifold.

TROUBLESHOOTING THE MECHANICAL PARTS OF THE ENGINE

Troubleshooting is performed before the engine is disassembled so that the mechanic can give the car owner an estimate of the cost of the repair job before work is started. This troubleshooting mate-

The spark plugs of an overchoked engine will be wet with fuel.

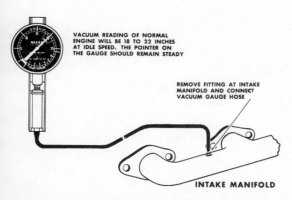

VACUUM READING OF NORMAL ENGINE WILL BE 18 TO 22 INCHES AT IDLE SPEED. THE POINTER ON THE GAUGE SHOULD REMAIN STEADY

REMOVE FITTING AT INTAKE MANIFOLD AND CONNECT VACUUM GAUGE HOSE

INTAKE MANIFOLD

A vacuum gauge is a very important testing device. It is connected to the intake manifold.

rial will also be useful in assisting a mechanic to solve those few minor defects which sometimes occur after a reconditioning job, even after meticulous care has been taken in rebuilding the engine. In most cases, it is just some little thing causing the engine to lose power, overheat, knock, pump oil, or lose compression.

Two very important gauges are needed to locate mechanical engine defects: a vacuum and a compression gauge. The vacuum gauge measures the amount of vacuum in the intake manifold and is an excellent indicator of the over-all efficiency of the engine. Many engine mechanical defects can be identified with a vacuum gauge. The compression gauge is used to identify the exact cylinder in which a compression defect exists.

USING A VACUUM GAUGE

The vacuum gauge is connected to the intake manifold through the windshield wiper hose fitting. The engine should be run until it is at operating temperature and then idled to obtain a reading.

CORRECTIONS. A vacuum gauge indicates the difference between the pressure inside the intake manifold and the atmospheric pressure outside. It is calibrated in inches of mercury (Hg). Consequently, the reading will be affected by any variation in atmospheric pressure, such as altitude and weather conditions; therefore, the most important thing about a vacuum gauge is the action of the needle rather than a theoretical numerical reading. Generally speaking, the vacuum gauge reading will be 1" lower for each 1000' of elevation.

NORMAL ENGINE. A normal engine will show a gauge reading of 18"–22" Hg with the pointer steady. Eight-cylinder engines will read toward the high side whereas 6- and 4-cylinder engines will read closer to the low side. On many later model cars, with overlapping valve timing, the gauge needle will fluctuate widely. To overcome this, many gauges have a constrictor valve which can be adjusted until the fluctuations are reduced

to the width of the pointer tip. On gauges without this valve, the hose can be pinched until the undesirable fluctuations cease.

LEAKING VALVE. If a valve is leaking, the pointer will drop from 1"–7" at regular intervals whenever the defective valve attempts to close during idle.

STICKING VALVE. A sticking valve is indicated by a rapid, intermittent drop each time the valve is supposed to close when the engine is idling. A sticky valve condition can be pinpointed by applying a small amount of penetrating oil or lacquer thinner to each guide in turn. When the sticky valve is reached, the situation will be remedied temporarily.

WEAK OR BROKEN VALVE SPRING. If the pointer fluctuates rapidly between 10"–22" Hg at 2,000 rpm, and the fluctuations increase as engine speed is increased, weak valve springs are indicated. If a valve spring is broken, the pointer will fluctuate rapidly every time the valve attempts to close at idle.

WORN VALVE GUIDES. Worn valve guides admit air which upsets carburetion. The vacuum gauge reading will be lower than normal with fluctuations of about 3" Hg on each side of normal when the engine is idling.

PISTON RING DEFECTS. Open the throttle and allow the engine to pick up speed to about 2,000 rpm, and then close the throttle quickly. The pointer should jump from about 2"–5" Hg or more above the normal reading if the rings are in good condition. A lower gain should be investigated by making a compression test to localize trouble.

BLOWN CYLINDER HEAD GASKET. The pointer will drop sharply 10" Hg from a normal reading and return each time the defective cylinders reach firing position with the engine idling.

INCORRECT IDLE AIR-FUEL MIXTURE. When the needle drifts slowly back and forth on idle, the fuel mixture is too rich. A lean mixture will cause an irregular drop of the needle.

INTAKE MANIFOLD AIR LEAKS. If there are any air leaks in the induction system, the needle will drop from 3"–9" Hg below normal with the engine idling, but will remain quite steady.

RESTRICTED EXHAUST SYSTEM. Open the throttle until about 2,000 rpm is reached. Close the throttle quickly. If there is no excessive back pressure, the pointer will drop to not less than 2", increase to 25" Hg, and then return to normal quickly. If the gauge does not register 5" Hg or more above the normal reading, and the needle seems to stop momentarily in its return, the exhaust system is partially restricted.

LATE IGNITION TIMING. A low steady reading on idle indicates late ignition timing or a uniformly close setting of the tappet adjustments. The timing must never be set with a vacuum gauge; use a timing light for accuracy.

LATE VALVE TIMING. A steady but very low

SOLENOID   COMPRESSION GAUGE

A compression gauge is important for checking the valve and ring condition. In practice, an equal number of pulses are recorded.

reading is generally caused by late ignition timing or late valve timing. If advancing the ignition timing does not increase the gauge reading to normal, then the valve timing is out of adjustment.

USING A COMPRESSION GAUGE

Another very important engine testing gauge is the compression tester. It measures the pressure within the cylinder in pounds per square inch (psi). As with the vacuum gauge, the theoretical numerical reading is not so important as the variation between cylinders. The cylinder pressures should not vary over 15 psi; otherwise, the engine cannot be tuned properly. Variations cause uneven idling and loss of power.

To use the gauge, remove all the spark plugs and insert the rubber tip into each spark plug hole in turn. With the throttle held wide open, crank the engine to obtain about 6 power impulses on the gauge; record the reading. Do this at each cylinder and compare the results. Generally, modern high-compression engines have a reading close to 175 psi. If one cylinder is low, insert a tablespoonful of heavy oil on top of the piston. Turn the engine over several times to work the oil around the piston rings, and then repeat the test. If the pressure shows a decided increase, there is a compression loss past the piston and rings. If the pressure does not increase, the valves are seating improperly. A defective cylinder head gasket will show a loss of compression in two adjacent cylinders.

LOW-COMPRESSION TROUBLESHOOTING CHART

TROUBLES & CAUSES

1. **Valves**
   1a. Insufficient tappet clearance
   1b. Sticking valves
   1c. Warped heads or bent stems
   1d. Burned, pitted, or distorted valve faces and seats
   1e. Weak or broken valve springs
   1f. Distortion of cylinder head and/or block caused by uneven tightening of the bolts
   1g. Incorrect valve timing
2. **Pistons and rings**
   2a. Excessive clearance between pistons and cylinder walls
   2b. Eccentric or tapered cylinder bores
   2c. Scored cylinder walls
   2d. Scored pistons
   2e. Broken pistons
   2f. Scuffed rings
   2g. Insufficient piston ring end gaps
   2h. Stuck piston rings
   2i. Binding of rings due to "set" caused by mechanic overstretching during installation
   2j. Insufficient piston ring-to-wall tension due to weak expanders
   2k. Ring lands worn unevenly
   2l. Ring grooves too deep for the expanders used
   2m. Standard rings installed in oversize bores
   2n. Top rings running dry because oil control rings are too severe
   2o. Top rings running dry because of gasoline dilution caused by stuck manifold heat control
   2p. Abrasive dust left in cylinder bores from honing or grinding valves
3. **Gaskets**
   3a. Warped head and/or block
   3b. Blown-out cylinder head gasket
   3c. Cylinder head bolts tightened unevenly
   3d. Incorrect type of gasket

TROUBLESHOOTING FOR EXCESSIVE OIL CONSUMPTION

Oil can be consumed in the combustion chamber or lost through leaks. If the engine is actually burning oil, a blue-gray smoke will emerge from the exhaust pipe whenever the engine is accelerated, especially after it has idled for a short period of time. Fouled spark plugs are a good indication that oil is being burned in the combustion chambers.

Oil can pass into the combustion areas in only 3 ways: it can go past the piston rings, past the valve guides, or it can pass through a defective crankcase ventilation system. Leaks can be caused by defective or improperly installed gaskets, by excessive crankcase pressures caused by blow-by, or by plugging of the crankcase ventilating system. Unless the vents are clean, blow-by pressures can force enough oil vapors from the crankcase to cause a noticeable increase in oil consumption.

OIL LEAKS

Fresh oil on any engine housing usually washes the dirt from that part and is an excellent indication that oil is leaking from that area. Washed

Oil leaks can be pinpointed by mixing a special fluorescent powder with the oil, and then shining a blacklight under the pan to locate the source of the leak.

areas on the ventilator side of the chassis usually are caused by oil being blown or sucked out of the crankcase. It is surprising just how much oil can be lost through a small leak. One drop of oil every hundred feet causes an oil loss of a quart per thousand miles. Note how the center of each driving lane is covered with oil from external leaks, and you will realize the need for checking this loss. Note that these drippings are much heavier on an upgrade due to blow-by pressures forcing the oil through defective gaskets and bearings.

CRANKCASE VENTILATOR

On road-draft type crankcase ventilating systems, clogged inlet breather caps and plugged vents in the outlet tube increase the crankcase pressures and so contribute to oil leaks.

Where a positive-type crankcase ventilating system is used, clogging of the metering valve, located in the line between the crankcase and the intake manifold, will cause crankcase pressure to increase, which will force the oil out from around the pan gaskets and oil seals. If the valve sticks open, large quantities of oil vapors will be drawn into the combustion areas under high-vacuum operating conditions with resulting high oil consumption.

Since oil can be lost in any combination of the above ways, it is necessary for the mechanic to examine the engine carefully before it is disassembled.

EXCESSIVE OIL CONSUMPTION TROUBLESHOOTING CHART

TROUBLES & CAUSES
1. **Piston and ring defects**
   1a. Piston improperly fitted or finished
   1b. Snaky piston ring grooves
   1c. Ring grooves worn overwidth or flared
   1d. Insufficient number of drain holes in oil ring grooves
   1e. Drain holes in oil ring grooves too small
   1f. Piston and connecting rod assembly out of alignment
   1g. Excessive clearance between piston and cylinder bore
   1h. Badly worn or collapsed pistons
   1i. Scuffed rings
   1j. Improper seating of rings in grooves
   1k. Insufficient clearance at ring gap
   1l. Insufficient ring tension
   1m. Out-of-round rings from improper installation
   1n. Warped or twisted rings from improper installation
   1o. Not enough side clearance between rings and grooves
   1p. Compression rings installed upside down
   1q. Wrong size rings
   1r. Insufficient ventilation in oil rings
   1s. Slots in oil rings clogged
2. **Bearing defects**
   2a. Scored rod bearings
   2b. Spurt holes in rods with worn bearings adding to excessive bearing throw-off
   2c. Worn crankshaft throws
   2d. Worn main bearing oil seals
   2e. Excessive clearance
3. **Valve guide defects**
   3a. Worn valve guides
   3b. Intake valve guides installed upside down
   3c. Valve stem oil seals incorrectly installed or worn
4. **Cylinder bore defects**
   4a. Excessively worn, tapered, or out-of-round cylinder bores
   4b. Wavy cylinder bores caused by heat distortion or uneven tightening of head bolts
   4c. Ring ledge at top or bottom of cylinder bore
   4d. Scored cylinder bores

The blacklight is moved about until the source of the leak is located by a glow as the lamp causes the oil to fluoresce.

4e. Rough finish on cylinder walls causing rapid ring wear

4f. Cylinder block out of alignment with crankshaft

5. Crankcase defects

5a. Main bearing oil return pipe clogged

5b. Oil level too high

5c. Broken pipe in oil line spraying oil into cylinder bores

5d. Clogged breather pipe

5e. Stuck valve in positive-type crankcase ventilating system

5f. Excessive crankcase pressures caused by blow-by

5g. Improper reading of dip stick (not pushed in fully)

TROUBLESHOOTING FOR ENGINE NOISES

One of the more difficult problems facing the mechanic is the locating of foreign noises. Engine noises vary in intensity and frequency, depending on their source. It is difficult to describe engine noises with mere words. Experience will have to be built up using the descriptions which follow as a guide.

The only tools which the mechanic has to help him locate the source of an engine noise are a screwdriver to short out spark plugs and a stethoscope or listening rod to carry the sound directly to his ear.

CRANKSHAFT KNOCKS

Noises classified as crankshaft knocks are usually dull, heavy metallic knocks which increase in frequency as the speed and load on the engine are increased. Or they may become more noticeable at extremely low speed when the engine is idling unevenly.

The most common crankshaft knock, due to excessive clearance, is usually apparent as an audible "bump" under the following conditions: when the engine is pulling hard, when an engine is started, during acceleration, or at speeds above 35 mph (56 km./h.). If excessive clearance exists at only one or two of the crankshaft journals, the "bump" will be less frequent and less pronounced. Usually, alternate short circuiting of each spark plug will determine the approximate location of a loose bearing.

Excessive crankshaft end-play causes a sharp rap to occur at irregular intervals, usually at idling speeds, and, in bad cases, can be detected by the alternate release and engagement of the clutch. To detect a loose flywheel, advance the engine idle to a road speed equivalent to 15 mph (24 km./h.). Turn off the ignition switch and, when the engine has almost stopped, turn the switch on again. If this operation is repeated several times and if, of course, the flywheel is loose, one distinct knock will be noted each time the switch is turned on.

CONNECTING ROD BEARING NOISES

Connecting rod bearing noises are usually a light rap or clatter of much less intensity than main bearing knocks. The noise is most audible when the engine is "floating" or running with a light load at approximately 25 mph (40 km./h.). The noise becomes louder as engine speed is increased. Connecting rod bearing knocks can be located best by grounding out each of the spark plugs, one at a time. Generally, the noise cannot be eliminated entirely by a short circuit, but ordinarily will be reduced considerably in intensity.

PISTON NOISES

The commonest piston noise is a slap due to the rocking of the piston from side to side in the cylinder. Although, in some engines, piston slap causes a clicking noise, usually it is a hollow, muffled, bell-like sound. Slight piston noises that occur when the engine is cold, and disappear after the engine is warm, do not ordinarily warrant correction. Piston ring noises generally cause a click, a snap, or a sharp rattle on acceleration.

Short circuit each spark plug in turn to locate piston and ring noises. As this test will affect other engine noises, sometimes the result is confusing. To detect piston slap more accurately, drive the car at low speeds under a load. The noise generally increases in intensity as the throttle is opened and additional load applied. On some engines, with very loose pistons, a piston rattle is encountered at speeds between 30–50 mph (48–80 km./h.) when the engine is not being accelerated.

To eliminate piston and ring noises momentarily, put 1–2 oz. (25–50 gr.) of very heavy engine oil into each cylinder through the spark plug hole. Crank the engine for several revolutions with the ignition switch turned off until the oil works itself down past the piston rings. Then install the spark plugs, start the engine, and determine whether or not the noise still exists.

A stethoscope or a listening rod is handy to locate the source of engine noises.

PISTON PIN NOISES

The commonest piston pin noise is the result of excessive piston pin clearance. This causes a sharp, metallic, double-knock, generally audible with the engine idling. On some engines, however, the noise is more noticeable at car speeds of 25–35 mph (40–56 km./h.). Interference between the upper end of the connecting rod and the pin boss (bossing) is difficult to diagnose and can be mistaken for a valve lifter noise.

To test for piston pin noises, allow the engine to run at idle speed. In most cases, a sharp metallic double-knock will become more evident when the spark plug, in the cylinder with the loose piston pin, is shorted out. Retarding the spark will generally reduce the intensity of the knock. If the pins in all pistons are loose, a metallic rattle, which is impossible to short out in any one cylinder, will be heard.

VALVE MECHANISM NOISES

Noisy valve mechanism has a characteristic clicking sound occurring at regular intervals. Inasmuch as the valves are operating at half crankshaft speed, the frequency of valve action noise is generally lower than that of other engine noises.

To determine whether the noise is due to excessive valve clearance, insert a feeler gauge between the valve stem and the rocker arm or tappet. If the noise stops, the clearance is probably excessive and the adjusting screw should be adjusted. Never reduce the clearance to below factory specification or the valve will burn.

A sticky valve will cause a clicking sound similar to a loose tappet adjustment which comes and goes according to driving conditions. A sticky valve can be detected by driving the car hard until the engine is well heated. Then quickly allow the engine to idle. If there is a sticky valve, the clicking will become quite pronounced but will lessen gradually and sometimes disappear as the engine returns to normal operating temperature. The noise is accompanied by a rhythmic jerk due to the misfiring cylinder. As the noise disappears, so does the jerk, and the engine will finally smooth out as the valve seats.

A loose timing gear generally can be detected by a sharp clatter at low engine speeds with an uneven idle. When testing for this condition, short circuit one or two spark plugs to produce the necessary rough idle.

SPARK KNOCK

Preignition, or spark knock, causes a metallic ringing sound, often described as a "ping." Usually, it is encountered when the engine is laboring, being accelerated rapidly, or is overheated. Preignition is caused by an incandescent particle of carbon or metal in the combustion chamber igniting the mixture prematurely while the piston is coming up on the compression stroke. This results in very heavy pressure being applied to the piston at the wrong time, causing the piston, the connecting rod, and the bearing to vibrate, and resulting in the sound known as "spark knock."

Detonation is caused most frequently by a fuel of too low an octane rating. It burns too rapidly, resulting in sudden and abnormal pressure against the piston.

ACCESSORY NOISES

Noises in the generator or water pump can be checked by removing the drive belt for a short operating period. If the noise remains, it is not in the generator or the water pump.

ENGINE NOISE TROUBLESHOOTING CHART

TROUBLES & CAUSES

1. **Crankshaft knocks**
   1a. Excessive bearing clearance
   1b. Excessive end-play
   1c. Eccentric or out-of-round journals
   1d. Sprung crankshaft
   1e. Bearing misalignment
   1f. Insufficient oil supply
   1g. Restricted oil supply to one main bearing
   1h. Low oil pressure
   1i. Badly diluted oil
   1j. Loose flywheel
   1k. Loose impulse neutralizer
   1l. Broken crankshaft web
2. **Connecting rod bearing knocks**
   2a. Excessive bearing clearance
   2b. Out-of-round crankpin journals
   2c. Misaligned connecting rods
   2d. Top of connecting rod bolt turned around and striking the camshaft
   2e. Insufficient oil supply
   2f. Low oil pressure
   2g. Badly diluted oil
3. **Piston noises**
   3a. Collapsed piston skirt
   3b. Excessive piston-to-cylinder bore clearance
   3c. Eccentric or tapered cylinder bores
   3d. Piston pin too tight
   3e. Connecting rod misalignment
   3f. Piston or rings hitting ridge at top of cylinder bore
   3g. Piston striking carbon accumulation at top of cylinder bore
   3h. Piston striking cylinder head gasket
   3i. Broken piston ring
   3j. Excessive side clearance between a ring and its groove
   3k. Piston pin hole out of square with the piston
   3l. Ring lands not properly relieved
4. **Piston pin noises**
   4a. Excessive piston pin clearance
   4b. Tight pin causing piston to slap

4c. Piston pin rubbing against cylinder wall
4d. Top end of connecting rod bossing

5. Valve mechanism noises
5a. Excessive clearance between valve stem and tappet or rocker arm
5b. Sticky valve
5c. Excessive clearance between tappet and block
5d. Lower end of lifter scored or broken
5e. Tappet screw or rocker arm face pitted
5f. Weak or broken valve spring
5g. Inverted valve spring
5h. Warped valve head
5i. Valve seat not concentric with guide
5j. Excessive stem-to-guide clearance
5k. End of valve stem not faced square
5l. Weak rocker arm spacer spring
5m. Loose timing gear

6. Spark knock
6a. Low octane fuel
6b. Excessive carbon deposits
6c. Ignition timed too early
6d. Excessively lean air-fuel mixture
6e. Weak automatic advance weight springs
6f. Manifold heat control valve stuck in closed position
6g. Spark plugs too hot
6h. Burned spark plug porcelain
6i. Sharp metallic edges in combustion chamber
6j. Cylinder head gasket projecting into combustion chamber
6k. Overheated valves
6l. Excessive engine coolant temperatures
6m. Loose fan belt

7. Accessory noises
7a. Defective generator bearings
7b. Loose generator drive pulley
7c. Brushes not seating
7d. Loose drive belt
7e. Defective water pump bearings
7f. Loose water pump drive pulley
7g. Bent and out-of-balance fan

TROUBLESHOOTING FOR POOR PERFORMANCE DUE TO EXCESSIVE FRICTION

Excessive friction is a frequent contributing cause of power losses; tight rings are perhaps the greatest offender. In an attempt to stop oil pumping, severe expander springs are frequently used behind piston rings. These rings create such excessive cylinder wall friction that power and gas mileage drop amazingly. The best test of a tight engine is to hold the throttle open to an engine speed of approximately 1,000 rpm. Keep the accelerator pedal steady and shut off the ignition. Watch the fan blades to see whether or not the engine rocks as it comes to a stop. A tight engine will stop with a "jerk" while a normal engine will rock back and forth on compression.

EXCESSIVE-FRICTION TROUBLESHOOTING CHART

TROUBLES & CAUSES

1. Engine conditions
1a. Piston ring expanders too severe
1b. Piston expanders too severe
1c. Piston slots not completed
1d. Wrong cam grind on pistons
1e. Insufficient piston-to-cylinder wall clearance
1f. Insufficient piston ring end gap
1g. Top ring lands not relieved
1h. Too tight a bearing fit

2. Miscellaneous conditions
2a. Dragging brakes
2b. Tight wheel bearings
2c. Misaligned wheels
2d. Underinflated tires

TROUBLESHOOTING THE COOLING SYSTEM

The cooling system is thermostatically controlled in some engines to regulate the engine operating temperature to provide for a short warm-up period. Engine overheating and slow warm-up are the two engine troubles most commonly attributed to the cooling system.

OVERHEATING

Loss of coolant, the accumulation of rust and scale in the coolant chambers, and the passing of hot exhaust gases into the coolant through an internal leak are the main causes of overheating.

Loss of coolant can be checked visually by the red rust stains that often form around the leak area. Loss of coolant through an internal crack is often detected by noting the condition of the oil on the dip stick, where water bubbles will appear with the oil. A newly developed method of testing for coolant leaks is to pour a water-soluble dye into the radiator. The dye contains a fluorescent powder which turns green when exposed to a special test lamp's rays.

The source of water leaks can also be pinpointed by the use of a special fluorescent powder that can be added to the coolant. A blacklight is used to pick up the leak.

By moving the special blacklight around, the exact point of the leak can be located.

TESTING FOR AN EXHAUST GAS LEAK

Start the test with a cold engine. Disconnect the fan belt so that the water pump does not operate. Disconnect the upper hose at the radiator. Drain the system until the water level is even with the top of the block. Remove the thermostat and replace the housing. Fill the radiator until the water reaches the top of the thermostat housing.

The object of this test is to place a load on the engine so that combustion chamber pressures approach maximum to force hot exhaust gases through any small leak that might exist.

To load the engine: jack up the rear wheels, start the engine, place the shift lever in high gear, open the accelerator wide with your right foot; at the same time apply the foot brakes with your left foot to hold the engine speed to about 20 mph (32 km./h.) road speed.

Gas bubbles or surging at the upper outlet indicate that exhaust gas is leaking into the cooling system. The test must be conducted quickly to prevent the coolant from boiling in the head.

Another method of testing the engine for leaks is to use a special radiator pressure pump. Drain some water until the level is about ½" (12 mm.) below the radiator neck. Attach the tester and apply 15 psi (1.0 kg./cm.²) pressure. If the pressure drops, check all points for an exterior leak.

If you cannot locate an exterior leak after the gauge shows a drop in pressure, detach the tester and run the engine to normalize it. Reattach the tester and pump it to 7 psi (0.5 kg./cm.²) while the engine is running. Race the engine and, if the dial fluctuates, it indicates a combustion leak. *CAUTION: Pressure builds up fast!* Never let the pressure exceed 15 psi (1.0 kg./cm.²). Release excess pressure immediately!

COOLING SYSTEM TROUBLESHOOTING CHART

TROUBLES & CAUSES

1. **Overheating**
   1a. Insufficient coolant
   1b. Rust and scale formations in cooling system
   1c. Fan belt slipping
   1d. Defective water pump
   1e. Rusted-out distributor tube
   1f. Radiator or hoses clogged
   1g. Radiator air flow restricted
   1h. Thermostat stuck closed
2. **Engine fails to reach normal operating temperature**
   2a. Thermostat defective
   2b. Temperature sending unit defective
   2c. Temperature indicator defective
3. **Slow warm-up**
   3a. Thermostat defective
   3b. Manifold heat control stuck open
   3c. Automatic choke not closing properly

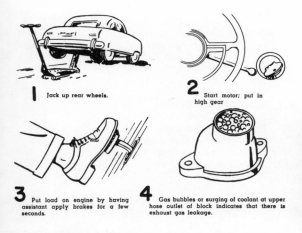

1 Jack up rear wheels.

2 Start motor; put in high gear

3 Put load on engine by having assistant apply brakes for a few seconds.

4 Gas bubbles or surging of coolant at upper hose outlet of block indicates that there is exhaust gas leakage.

To test for a crack in the block or head, which lets hot exhaust gases pass through the coolant, place a load on the engine and check for exhaust bubbles at the top water hose casting.

To check a cooling system for leaks, it can be pressurized by this special pump, and then the gauge can be checked to see whether the system holds the pressure.

4. Loss of coolant
    4a. Leaking radiator
    4b. Loose or damaged hose connections
    4c. Defective water pump
    4d. Cylinder head gasket defective or loose
    4e. Uneven tightening of cylinder head bolts
    4f. Cracked block or head
    4g. Pressure cap defective

TROUBLESHOOTING THE FUEL SYSTEM

The fuel system furnishes a combustible air-fuel mixture to each cylinder. Failure of the fuel system to function properly can result in various complaints: hard starting, poor performance, and excessive fuel consumption.

HARD STARTING

An engine may not start because of either too much or not enough fuel in the combustion chamber. Too much fuel can be caused by percolation or overchoking. Insufficient fuel may be the result of a defective fuel pump, a restricted line, a porous flexible line, a plugged gas tank vent, or an empty gas tank.

A quick test of the fuel system is to move the throttle back and forth while looking down into the carburetor bore. If fuel is present it will be squirted out into the throat of the carburetor. If overchoking is suspected, the accelerator pedal should be advanced to a wide-open position while the engine is cranked to admit more air. Do not pump the pedal or you will force more liquid fuel into the intake manifold and aggravate the condition.

POOR PERFORMANCE

Loss of power, resulting from defects in the fuel system, is due to an air-fuel mixture that is either too lean or too rich.

Lean Mixture. The most commonly experienced fuel system trouble is a pause or "flat spot" on acceleration. If such a condition exists, check the operation of the accelerating pump system in the carburetor. To check the carburetor, remove the air cleaner and move the throttle back and forth. A stream of fuel should flow from the accelerating jet if the system is functioning properly. If the fuel stream is missing completely, thin, deflected to one side, or merely dribbling out, the carburetor must be overhauled.

Another lean condition may result from too little fuel being supplied by the carburetor during the range period of operation. Such a condition gives a feeling of "mushiness" as the throttle is opened gradually; the engine doesn't seem to respond. In severe cases, the engine may backfire through the carburetor.

A lean condition can also result from a weak fuel pump or a restricted gas line. Generally, the

A lean fuel mixture will cause excessively high combustion chamber temperatures, which generally result in spark plug and valve burning.

engine seems to run out of fuel at a certain road speed when there are defects in the supply line.

Rich Mixture. A rich mixture will also cause a loss of power. Excessive quantities of fuel will not vaporize and burn completely. Liquid fuels wash the lubricant from the cylinder walls, allowing the rings to make metal-to-metal contact. Scuffed rings and excessive oil and fuel consumption result.

A rich mixture may result from high fuel pump pressure which forces the carburetor needle valve off its seat, causing flooding. It also can result from defects in the automatic choke.

FUEL SYSTEM TROUBLESHOOTING CHART

TROUBLES & CAUSES

1. Mixture too lean
    1a. Manifold air leaks
    1b. Defective fuel pump
    1c. Defective carburetor
    1d. Clogged fuel line
    1e. Clogged fuel filter
    1f. Flexible gas line leaking
    1g. Plugged tank vent
2. Mixture too rich
    2a. Defective carburetor
    2b. Defective automatic choke
    2c. Carburetor percolating
    2d. Fuel pump pressure too high
3. No fuel in carburetor
    3a. Gas tank empty
    3b. Fuel pump defective
    3c. Clogged fuel filter
    3d. Vapor lock
    3e. Air leak at fuel pump inlet fitting or porous flexible hose
    3f. Fuel line kinked or plugged
    3g. Fuel vent closed
    3h. Carburetor needle valve stuck in seat by gum

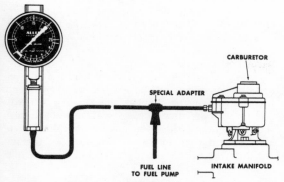

A pressure gauge can be hooked into the fuel line with a "T" fitting to test the pump operating pressure.

TESTING THE FUEL PUMP

A fuel pump must be tested for both capacity and pressure. The pressure test is made to check for excessively low or high pressures. Low pressure indicates that the pump stroke is relatively short—an indication of worn linkage. High pressure can be caused only by installing the wrong pump or the wrong pump pressure spring during rebuilding. High pressure causes the float bowl level to rise, which enriches the mixture proportionately. In some cases, high pressure forces the needle valve off its seat and causes the carburetor to flood.

Road Test. A good quick road test of the efficiency of the fuel system is to run the car at high speed while keeping the shift lever in second gear. A good fuel pump will permit the car to attain speeds up to and above 50 mph (80 km./h.) in second gear. A defective fuel pump will permit the car to attain a high speed but then it will slow down rapidly.

The test results should not be confused with similar results obtained with a defective ignition system which will allow the car to attain a critical speed, and will maintain it regardless of additional throttle pressure, while a defective fuel pump will cause the car to slow down rapidly after the carburetor runs out of fuel.

TROUBLESHOOTING THE ELECTRIC FUEL PUMP

A pump in good condition will pump 1 pint (0.57 litre) per minute. If the pump is weak or does not work at all, it can be checked out as follows: (1) Test the battery supply by turning on the ignition switch and checking for current with the wire disconnected from the pump terminal. (2) If there is current at the wire, but the pump does not work, remove the bakelite cover and touch the hot wire to both contact points in turn. If the pump operates with current supplied to the bottom point, but not when it is supplied to the top, then the contact points are dirty. They

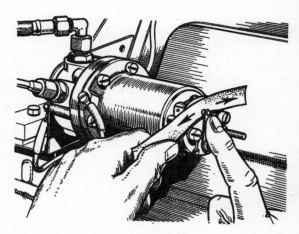

Cleaning the contact points of the electric fuel pump with sandpaper.

can be cleaned by passing a sheet of sandpaper through the points while holding them closed. Finish with a piece of cardboard to remove all traces of sand which could hold the points apart. (3) Check to see that the points open and close when the carburetor float depressing plunger is pushed in. This releases pressure on the output line so that the pump should operate. (4) If the pump operates noisily and rapidly, it is an indication that there is an air leak in the line from the tank. (5) If the pump operates without delivering fuel, one of the valves is not seating. (6) If the pump operates, but works hard and overheats, it is probable that the filter is clogged.

ELECTRIC FUEL PUMP TROUBLESHOOTING CHART

CAUTION: When bench testing the fuel pump, extinguish all flames in the vicinity and do not allow the cables to spark when making connections.

1. **Not enough fuel**
   1a. Check the level of the fuel in the tank.
   1b. Check the fuse.
   1c. If replacement fuse blows, check for a short circuit in the feed cable or the pump unit.
   1d. If fuse has not blown, locate the cable connectors located in the spare wheel compartment and check the voltage and current available at the terminal ends with the ignition switched ON. The voltage should be 12 volts and the current should not exceed 1.8 amperes.
   1e. If no voltage appears, check for an intermittent connection in the switch, feed, or ground.
   1f. If no current or an excessive current measurement is shown, the pump is defective.
2. **Too much fuel**
   2a. Defective carburetor needle valve.
   2b. Check the output pressure at the carburetor which should be between 2–2.5 psi (0.14–0.17 kg/cm^2).

TROUBLESHOOTING THE CARBURETOR

Each S.U. carburetor has a piston-lifting pin (*arrow*) for checking the fuel-air ratio. To check the mixture, lift the piston about 1/32″ with the lifting pin, or with a screwdriver inserted in the air intake port. The engine should speed up momentarily slightly if the mixture is correctly adjusted. If the engine speed increases and continues to run faster, the mixture is too rich. If the engine speed decreases, the mixture is too lean.

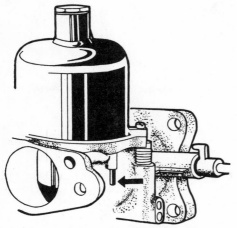

The pin (arrow) lifts the piston for checking the mixture.

S. U. CARBURETOR TROUBLESHOOTING CHART

1. Lean fuel mixture
   1a. Main jet adjusted too lean
   1b. Wrong air valve spring
   1c. Dirt in main jet
   1d. Too little oil in damper reservoir
   1e. Fuel pump pressure too low
   1f. Needle valve sticking
2. Flooding
   2a. Dirt in needle valve and seat
   2b. Defective needle valve and seat
   2c. Heavy float
3. Leaking
   3a. Diaphragm defective
4. Sticking piston
   4a. Dry piston rod
   4b. Dirt between the piston and rod

S. U. CARBURETOR TROUBLESHOOTING HINTS

PISTON STICKING
   The piston rod slides in a bearing in the center of the suction chamber which may gum up and affect carburetor performance. It can be checked by removing the dashpot piston damper, inserting your finger into the air intake, and lifting up the piston. When released, the piston should fall freely onto its seat. If sticking does occur, remove the assembly, clean it, and lubricate the piston rod. *CAUTION: No oil must be used on any other part of the piston assembly.*

WATER OR DIRT
   Should a particle of dirt stick between the jet and needle, it can be flushed out by pushing on the float-depressing plunger and flooding the carburetor. If the dirt cannot be flushed out, start the engine, open the throttle wide, and hold your hand over the air intake. If this does not remove the dirt, the carburetor must be disassembled and cleaned.

FLOAT CHAMBER FLOODING
   If gasoline flows from the air intake, the needle valve is not seating. Generally, this is due to particles of dirt between the needle and seat. Press on the float-depressing plunger to flood the carburetor which will generally flush out the dirt. Should leaking continue, the needle and seat assembly should be replaced.

FLOAT NEEDLE STICKING
   Sometimes the needle will stick to the seat because of gum formation. If the engine stops from lack of fuel, and the fuel pump output is satisfactory with the inlet pipe to the carburetor disconnected, the probable cause is sticking of the needle. Remove the float chamber lid to clean the gum. Be sure to clean the rest of the system to remove all gum or it will occur again.

MIXTURE CONTROL FAILING TO LOCK
   On some later models a mixture control, having a radial movement of 90°, is fitted. To ensure proper functioning of the device, it is important that the cable be given an initial twist of one-half turn in a clockwise direction, looking at the end of the cable, before the clamp is tightened.

TROUBLESHOOTING THE ELECTRICAL SYSTEM

The battery is the heart of the electrical system; it supplies the entire system with the current it needs to function. The generator charges the battery and develops the voltage or pressure on which the rest of the electrical system must work. The operation of all units is so interrelated that the improper functioning of any one will generally cause a malfunction in the others. For this reason, it is customary to make a series of tests to determine the condition of the entire electrical system to make sure that all troubles have been uncovered. All authorities recommend that the electrical system be tested in the following order: cranking circuit, charging circuit, and then the ignition circuit. In each case, the battery should be tested first because its condition determines the operating

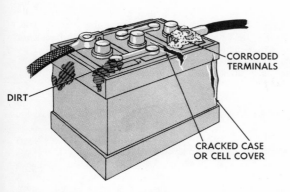

DIRT

CORRODED TERMINALS

CRACKED CASE OR CELL COVER

A visual inspection is often helpful in discovering battery defects.

voltage of the entire electrical system of the car, and it is a functional part of each basic circuit.

TROUBLESHOOTING THE BATTERY

Two battery tests are generally performed; one has to do with the chemical condition of the electrolyte, and the second with the capacity of the battery to deliver the necessary quantities of electricity.

The electrolyte test is made with a hydrometer which measures the density of the fluid. As a battery becomes discharged, a chemical reaction takes place in which the heavy sulfuric acid combines with the lead of the plates. As the sulfuric acid leaves the electrolyte, the solution contains more water than acid. This lightens the density, which can be measured by a hydrometer; a reading of 1.270 indicates a fully charged battery, one of 1.175 a battery low in charge.

If the battery capacity test indicates low, but the cell voltage readings are even, but low, the state of the battery charge is low, and it should be recharged.

BATTERY TROUBLESHOOTING CHART

TROUBLES & CAUSES

1. **Low specific gravity readings**
   1a. Low state of charge
   1b. Loss of acid through leaks
   1c. Acid absorbed by spongy plates
   1d. Sulfated plates
   1e. Electrical drain due to acid resistance path on top of the case or to a short circuit in the car wiring
2. **Low individual cell voltage readings**
   2a. Low state of charge
   2b. Loss of acid through a leak
   2c. Shorted plates caused by a defective separator
3. **Low current capacity**
   3a. Low state of charge
   3b. Sulfated plates
   3c. Low fluid level
   3d. Acid absorbed by spongy plates

ENGINE WILL NOT CRANK

TEST AND RECHARGE OR REPLACE BATTERY

CHECK STARTER RELAY

RELAY DOES NOT CLICK

RELAY CLICKS

STARTER SPINS

CHECK IGNITION SWITCH AND STARTER RELAY AND INSPECT WIRING. REPAIR OR REPLACE

CHECK STARTER DRIVE

★ TROUBLE OVER

★ TROUBLE OVER

CONNECT JUMPER ACROSS STARTER RELAY

ENGINE DOES NOT CRANK

ENGINE CRANKS

CHECK CONNECTIONS AND CABLES, CHECK FOR LOCKED STARTER-DRIVE OR HYDROSTATIC LOCK. REPAIR OR REPLACE

REPLACE RELAY

★ TROUBLE OVER

★ TROUBLE OVER

Roadmap for troubleshooting a starting motor that does not crank the engine.

3e. Powdered-out positive plates from overcharging
3f. Replacement battery too small for vehicle demands

TROUBLESHOOTING THE CRANKING SYSTEM

The condition of the cranking system has a decided effect on the ease of starting the engine—or the lack of it. A good cranking system will spin the engine fast enough to draw in a full combustible

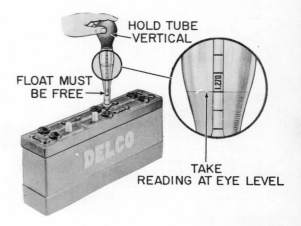

HOLD TUBE VERTICAL

FLOAT MUST BE FREE

TAKE READING AT EYE LEVEL

A hydrometer is used to measure the specific gravity of the electrolyte.

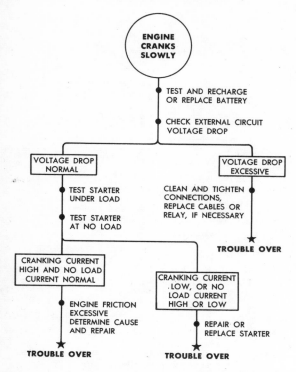

Roadmap for troubleshooting a starting motor that cranks the engine too slowly.

charge, compress it high enough to develop sufficient heat to dry out most of the wet fuel particles, and maintain a sufficiently high battery voltage so that the ignition system can operate efficiently.

Any defect in the cranking circuit slows down the cranking speed. And, because the starting motor fields and armature are connected in series, a slower speed allows more time for the current to flow through each armature coil which increases the current drain on the system. In turn, this lowers the battery voltage available to the ignition system which then operates at less than maximum efficiency. Thus, a vicious cycle is set up which results in a hard starting complaint.

CRANKING SYSTEM TROUBLESHOOTING CHART

TROUBLES & CAUSES

1. **Cranks engine slowly**
   1a. Low state of battery charge
   1b. High resistance battery cable connection
   1c. High resistance starter switch
   1d. Bent armature shaft
   1e. Worn bushing in the drive end
   1f. Dirty or worn commutator
   1g. Worn brushes or weak brush springs
2. **Doesn't crank the engine at all**
   2a. Dead battery
   2b. Broken battery cable or high resistance connection
   2c. Open circuit in the ignition-to-solenoid circuit

2d. Open circuit in the starting switch
2e. Open circuit in the starting motor
2f. Starting motor drive stuck to the flywheel gear
2g. Hydrostatic lock
3. **Spins, but does not crank the engine**
   3a. Defective starter drive

TROUBLESHOOTING THE CHARGING SYSTEM

Modern automotive charging systems have a regulator to control the output of the generator or alternator. In practice, the charging rate increases when the battery is discharged and decreases when it is charged. The charging rate may be cut down to a very low rate with a fully charged battery.

To test the charging system, crank the engine with the ignition switch off in order to discharge the battery slightly. (On cars with an ignition key-type starter switch, it may be necessary to remove the coil high tension wire from the center of the distributor cap to prevent the engine from starting.) Now, start the engine and note the charging rate. (On a car without an ammeter, it is necessary to insert an ammeter in the charging circuit.) As the engine is run for a short period, the charging rate should decrease with a properly operating regulator. If the ammeter does not show any charge after the above test, it is an indication that either the generator or the regulator is at fault.

To isolate the trouble, disconnect the regulator from the circuit and energize the generator field. If the generator now charges, the trouble is in the regulator. If the generator does not charge with the regulator out of the circuit and the field energized, then the trouble is in the generator. In every case in which the generator is burned out, the regulator should be replaced too, as it obviously did not control the output of the generator. *CAUTION: Do not race the engine with the regulator out of the circuit, or the generator will burn up as it is operating without control.*

Because several manufacturers supply electrical equipment for European-built cars, the method of energizing the field is detailed according to the type of generator supplied as follows:

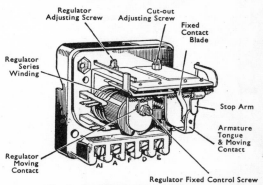

The Lucas RB 106/2 regulator.

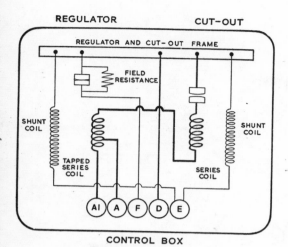

REGULATOR   CUT-OUT

REGULATOR AND CUT-OUT FRAME

FIELD RESISTANCE

SHUNT COIL

SHUNT COIL

TAPPED SERIES COIL

SERIES COIL

AI A F D E

CONTROL BOX

Internal wiring of the RB 106/2 regulator.

Bosch: Connect a jumper wire from the field terminal on the generator or the regulator to ground.

Ducellier: Connect a jumper wire from the EXC terminal on the regulator to the DYN terminal.

Fiat: Connect a jumper wire from No. 15 to No. 67 terminals on the regulator.

Lucas: Connect a jumper from the D terminal to the F terminal on the regulator.

Marelli: On 2-unit regulators, connect a jumper from the DF terminal on the regulator to ground. On the 3-unit regulators, connect a jumper between the DF-1 terminal and the D+ 61 terminal.

Paris-Rhone: Connect a jumper wire from the EXC terminal on the regulator to the DYN terminal.

If the generator output is excessive, the trouble can be caused by the regulator points being welded together or by a short circuit in a field wire. In either case, there is no regulation, and the generator is running wide open. To test for this type of trouble, it must be remembered that there are two basic types of field circuits: one grounded at the regulator and one supplied with current at the regulator. By removing the field wire from the regulator, the generator can be isolated. If the generator still charges with the field wire removed, then the ground or short is in the generator itself.

Another generator check can be made by removing the cover band. If the inner surface of the band is covered with a layer of solder, the generator was overloaded until the solder from the armature commutator slots melted. Obviously, this leads to open circuited coils in the armature. The wires can be resoldered and the commutator turned, provided that the coils have not grounded out; otherwise, the armature should be replaced.

Voltage losses, due to poor connections, cause an increase of operating voltage because the generator tries to overcome the added resistance of the circuit by forcing current through at a higher voltage. When the voltage increases, the regulator senses it and returns it to normal by regulating the field. Thus, even though the battery is low in charge, the generator output remains low, and another vicious cycle is set up.

CHARGING SYSTEM TROUBLESHOOTING CHART

TROUBLES & CAUSES

1. **Battery requires water too frequently**
   1a. Voltage regulator set too high
   1b. Current regulator set too high
   1c. Cracked battery case
2. **Battery will not remain charged**
   2a. Voltage regulator set too low
   2b. Current regulator set too low
   2c. Short circuit in car wiring
   2d. High-resistance connection in charging circuit
   2e. Excessive low-speed driving while operating accessories
   2f. Defective battery
   2g. Defective generator
   2h. Defective regulator
3. **Battery will not accept a charge**
   3a. Sulfated battery
   3b. Open circuit between cells
4. **Generator has no output**
   4a. Defective generator
   4b. Defective regulator
   4c. Grounded or open lead from armature terminal of generator or regulator
   4d. Ground or open circuit in the field lead
   4e. Field or ground wires reversed on generator
5. **Generator output low**
   5a. Slipping fan belt
   5b. Voltage regulator set too low
   5c. Current regulator set too low

ROUGH COMMUTATOR

A rough commutator surface is a sure indication of trouble in the making.

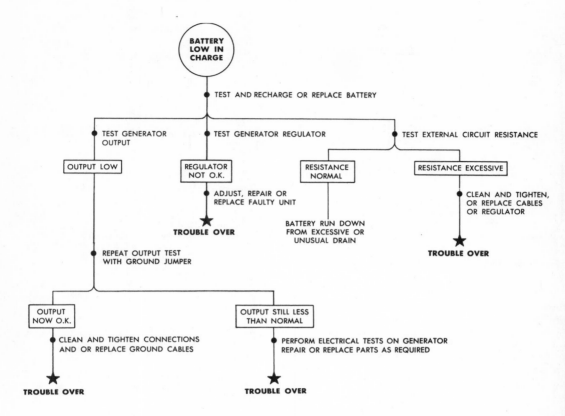

Roadmap for troubleshooting the charging circuit.

5d. High resistance in field circuit
5e. Defective generator

6. Generator output too high
6a. Voltage regulator set too high
6b. Current regulator set too high
6c. Defective regulator
6d. Ground or short in field lead

7. Voltage or current regulator points badly burned
7a. Shorted generator field windings
7b. Radio condenser connected to field terminal

8. Cutout points chatter
8a. Generator polarity reversed
8b. Battery installed in reverse
8c. Cutout relay closing voltage set too low

9. Noises
9a. Bad bearings
9b. Loose generator drive pulley
9c. Brushes not seating
9d. Loose fan belt

TROUBLESHOOTING THE IGNITION SYSTEM

The efficient operation of the ignition system probably has a great deal more to do with the smooth operation of an internal combustion engine than any other mechanical or electrical part. The importance of the ignition system can be realized from the fact that every minute 20,000 sparks are developed and delivered to the spark plugs of an 8-cylinder engine running at high speed. And, that these sparks must be distributed to each of the cylinders when they have been charged with an explosive air-fuel mixture that has been compressed to the point of maximum efficiency. Naturally, any slipup in the chain of events needed to create and time the sparks will result in poor engine performance.

The spark needed to fire the compressed air-fuel mixture is close to 20,000 volts. To step up the battery's 12 volts to the high voltage needed to jump the gaps of the spark plugs is the duty of the ignition coil. This transformer contains a primary and a secondary winding. The primary circuit, operating on the battery voltage, consists of the battery, ignition switch, ignition contact points, condenser, primary winding of the ignition coil, and ballast resistor. The secondary circuit develops the high voltage needed to fire the spark plugs, and it consists of the ignition coil, rotor, distributor cap, high tension wiring, and spark plugs.

The primary circuit contains a set of contact points which interrupts the circuit. The action of interrupting the primary circuit develops the high-tension spark in the secondary circuit. At the same time, the contact-point interruption is precisely

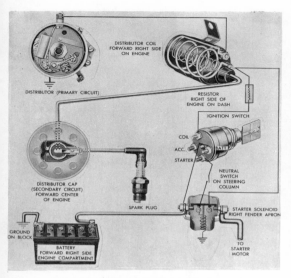

Pictorial diagram of the ignition system.

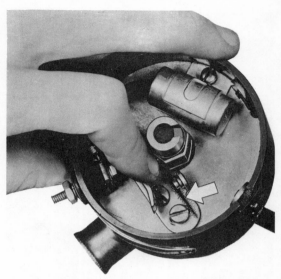

Oil on the contact point faces is a frequent offender of burned points. Its presence can often be detected by the smudge line under the contact points.

timed so as to send the spark to the cylinder at the instant the air-fuel charge has been compressed to the point of maximum efficiency. Naturally, the contact point set must open and close once for each spark delivered, or 20,000 times per minute at top speed. It is no wonder, then, that the contact points require periodic servicing. Without it, they soon deteriorate and cause such troubles as hard starting, misfiring, poor performance, and low fuel mileage.

There is no way to test the performance of the ignition system with accuracy except with precision test equipment. Any other way is subject to error. However, a rough check can be made of the ignition system by road testing the car while placing the engine under a heavy load. Drive the car in high gear at about 6 mph (10 km./h.) on a smooth road; place your left foot lightly on the brake pedal to put a load on the engine. Open the accelerator fully with your right foot. As the engine picks up speed, apply the foot brake to keep the car speed constant at about 25 mph (40 km./h.). Ignition troubles will cause the car to jerk sharply. Defective spark plugs are especially sensitive to such a test.

If the car can be driven wide open in second gear, a good ignition system will allow the car to attain a maximum speed. A defective ignition system will cause it to "float" long before it reaches maximum.

TESTING THE IGNITION SYSTEM FOR CONDITIONS CAUSING POWER LOSSES

Two common ignition system troubles, with regard to power losses, are late ignition timing and misfiring cylinders.

Late ignition timing causes overheating and loss of power. It can be detected by too smooth an idle, a deep-sounding exhaust, a low vacuum gauge reading, and a lack of "ping" on acceleration. Misfiring cylinders are characterized by a rough idle, a stuttering exhaust on acceleration, and a jerky vacuum gauge needle.

CHECKING IGNITION TIMING

A timing light should be used to check the ignition timing. One of the test instrument leads is connected to the distributor primary terminal and the other to ground. With the ignition switch turned on, the engine should be rotated by hand until the lamp lights, which indicates the moment of point opening.

Generally, the crankshaft pulley has a notch to indicate TDC (top dead center), and it is necessary to measure along the edge of the pulley to locate the exact point that ignition must occur. In many cases, no timing or degree scale is provided. The ignition timing specification can be found in the Commonly Used Specifications table according to car model.

To set the timing, turn the engine by hand until the pointer is at the exact point on the flywheel specified in the table. Loosen the distributor clamp bolt, and then turn the distributor in a direction opposite that of normal rotation until the points just separate (timing lamp lights). Lock the distributor in this position.

TESTING FOR A MISS

An engine is composed of several cylinders arranged to fire successively in order to develop a smooth flow of power. If one of these cylinders does not fire, it causes the engine to jerk, lose

TIMING LIGHT   DISTRIBUTOR

A timing light is used to check the moment of point opening. With the engine positioned at the specified point, adjust the position of the distributor until the lamp lights.

power, and waste fuel. A misfiring cylinder can be caused by a lack of spark, fuel, or compression.

The best test for a misfiring cylinder is to short out all the cylinders with the exception of one, and thereafter have the engine operate on each cylinder in turn. Any variation in power, or a cylinder which is not firing, will show up, because the engine will not run at all when the defective cylinder has to carry the load alone.

To make this test, loosen each high tension wire from its spark plug terminal before starting the engine, but do not disconnect any until needed. With the engine running fast enough to prevent stalling, short out each cylinder, except number 1, by removing its spark plug wire and laying it on the engine block. This is done so that the spark does not reach the spark plug and the cylinder cannot fire. To minimize the chances of getting an electrical shock when handling high tension wires, keep your fingers at least an inch from the metallic tip.

After all the cylinders, except one, have been shorted out, adjust the engine speed so that the engine runs as slowly as possible without stalling. Change the wires, one at a time. In this way, you can run the engine on each cylinder in turn. If a vacuum gauge is connected during this test, a very accurate comparative measurement can be made between the relative efficiency of each cylinder.

To Find the Cause of the Miss. Remove the defective cylinder spark plug wire; hold it 1/4" (6 mm.) from the spark plug terminal, then start the engine. If a steady spark jumps to the spark plug terminal, the trouble must be fuel, compression, or a defective spark plug. If no spark jumps to the spark plug terminal, the trouble is in the ignition system.

To make a compression test, use a compression gauge or hold your thumb over the spark plug hole while cranking the engine.

If the engine misses on adjacent cylinders, the trouble may be a blown cylinder head gasket or a leaky intake manifold gasket. A blown cylinder head gasket will lack compression in either of the two affected cylinders. To test for a leaking intake manifold gasket, squirt water around the suspected surfaces. A sucking noise will indicate the entrance of the water into the manifold.

IGNITION SYSTEM TROUBLESHOOTING CHART

TROUBLES & CAUSES

1. **Primary circuit troubles causing misfiring or hard starting**
   1a. Defective contact points
   1b. Point dwell not set correctly
   1c. Defective condenser
   1d. Defective coil
   1e. Defective primary wire in distributor
   1f. Resistance contacts in ignition switch
   1g. Discharged battery
   1h. Low voltage due to resistance connections
   1i. Worn distributor shaft bushings
2. **Secondary circuit troubles causing misfiring or hard starting**
   2a. Defective spark plugs
   2b. Spark plug gaps set too wide
   2c. Defective high tension wiring
   2d. Cracked distributor cap
   2e. Defective rotor
   2f. Defective coil
   2g. Moisture on the ignition wires, cap, or spark plugs
3. **Ignition troubles causing poor acceleration**
   3a. Ignition timing incorrect
   3b. Centrifugal advance incorrect
   3c. Vacuum advance unit incorrect
   3d. Defective vacuum advance diaphragm
   3e. Preignition due to wrong heat-range spark plugs, or to overheated engine
   3f. Spark plug gaps set too wide
   3g. Defective spark plugs
   3h. Cracked distributor cap
   3i. Weak coil
4. **Ignition troubles causing erratic engine operation**
   4a. Defective contact points
   4b. Sticking point pivot bushing
   4c. Worn distributor shaft bushings
   4d. Worn advance plate bearing
   4e. Defective ignition coil
   4f. Spark plug gaps set too wide
   4g. High resistance spark plugs
   4h. Defective high tension wiring

TROUBLESHOOTING THE CLUTCH

To test a clutch for slipping, set the hand brake tightly, open the throttle until the engine is running at about 30 mph (48 km./h.) road speed, depress the clutch pedal, and shift into high gear. Now, release the clutch; the engine should stall if the clutch is good. If the clutch is slipping, the engine will continue to run.

Check to see that the slipping is not due to a tight adjustment of the clutch pedal linkage. There must be ¾" (20 mm.) free play at the pedal, before the clutch thrust bearing contacts the clutch pressure plate levers.

The only other clutch trouble is chattering when starting in first or reverse gear. Loose engine mounts and uneven clutch finger adjustments contribute to this trouble.

CLUTCH TROUBLESHOOTING CHART

TROUBLES & CAUSES

1. **Slipping**
   1a. Worn facings
   1b. Weak pressure plate springs
   1c. Pedal linkage out of adjustment
   1d. Sticking release levers
   1e. Pressure plate binding against the drive lugs
2. **Dragging**
   2a. Pedal linkage adjustment too loose
   2b. Warped clutch disc
   2c. Splined hub sticking on clutch shaft
   2d. Torn disc facings
   2e. Release fingers adjusted unevenly
   2f. Sticking pilot bearing
   2g. Sticking release sleeve
   2h. Warped pressure plate
   2i. Misalignment of clutch housing
3. **Noise**
   3a. Clutch release bearing requires lubrication
   3b. Pilot bearing requires lubrication
   3c. Loose hub in clutch disc
   3d. Worn release bearing
   3e. Worn driving pins in pressure plate
   3f. Uneven release lever adjustment
   3g. Release levers require lubrication
4. **Chattering**
   4a. Oil or grease on clutch disc facings
   4b. Glazed linings
   4c. Warped clutch disc
   4d. Warped pressure plate
   4e. Sticking release levers
   4f. Unequal adjustment of release levers
   4g. Uneven pressure plate spring tension
   4h. Loose engine mounts
   4i. Loose splines on clutch hub
   4j. Loose universal joints or torque mountings
   4k. Misalignment of clutch housing

TROUBLESHOOTING A TRANSMISSION

Transmission noises can be heard much better with the engine shut off and the car coasting. By moving the shift lever from neutral into the various gearing positions, different gears can be meshed for testing purposes.

TRANSMISSION TROUBLESHOOTING CHART

TROUBLES & CAUSES

1. **Noisy with car in motion, any gear**
   1a. Insufficient lubrication
   1b. Worn clutch gear
   1c. Worn clutch gear bearing
   1d. Worn countergear
   1e. Worn countershaft bearings
   1f. Worn mainshaft rear bearing
   1g. Worn mainshaft front bearing
   1h. Worn sliding gears
   1i. Excessive mainshaft end play
   1j. Speedometer gears worn
   1k. Misalignment between transmission and clutch housing
2. **Noisy in neutral**
   2a. Insufficient lubrication
   2b. Worn clutch gear
   2c. Worn clutch gear bearing
   2d. Worn countergear drive gear
   2e. Worn countershaft bearings
3. **Slips out of high gear**
   3a. Misalignment between transmission and clutch housings
   3b. Worn shift detent parts
   3c. Worn clutch shaft bearing
   3d. Worn teeth on dog clutch
   3e. Improper adjustment of shift linkage
4. **Slips out of second gear**
   4a. Misalignment between transmission and clutch housings
   4b. Weak shift lever interlock detent springs
   4c. Worn mainshaft bearings
   4d. Worn clutch shaft bearing
   4e. Worn countergear thrust washers allowing too much end play
   4f. Improper adjustment of shift linkage
5. **Slips out of first/reverse gear**
   5a. Worn detent parts
   5b. Improper adjustment of shift linkage
   5c. Worn mainshaft bearings
   5d. Worn clutch shaft bearing
   5e. Excessive mainshaft end play
   5f. Worn countergear
   5g. Worn countergear bearings
   5h. Worn first/reverse sliding gear
6. **Difficult to shift**
   6a. Clutch not releasing
   6b. Improper adjustment of shift linkage
7. **Clashing when shifting**
   7a. Worn synchronizing cones
   7b. Excessive mainshaft end play
8. **Backlash**
   8a. Excessive mainshaft end play
   8b. Excessive countergear end play
   8c. Broken mainshaft bearing retainer
   8d. Worn mainshaft bearing

TROUBLESHOOTING THE REAR AXLE

A rear axle should not be disassembled until a thorough diagnosis is made of the trouble and symptoms observed during the operation of the car. The most common rear axle complaint is noise. Care must be taken to be sure that the noise is not caused by the engine, tires, transmission, wheel bearings, or some other part of the car.

Before road testing the car, make sure that sufficient lubricant is in the axle housing and inflate the tires to the correct pressure. Drive the car far enough to warm the lubricant to its normal operating temperature before making the tests.

Engine noise or exhaust noise can be detected by parking the car and running the engine at various speeds with the transmission in neutral. A portable tachometer will assist in duplicating road speeds at which the noises occurred.

Tire noise can be detected by driving the car over various road surfaces. Tire noise is minimized on smooth asphalt or black-top roads. Switching tires can help to detect or eliminate tire noises.

Wheel bearing noise can sometimes be detected by jacking up each wheel in turn and feeling for roughness as the wheel is rotated. Wheel bearing noise is most obvious on a low-speed coast. Applying the brakes lightly while the car is moving will often reduce or eliminate the noise caused by a defective wheel bearing.

A car should be tested for axle and driveline noise by operating it under four driving conditions:

1. Drive: Higher than normal road-load power, where the speed gradually increases on level road acceleration.

2. Cruise: Constant speed operation at normal road speeds.

3. Float: Using only enough throttle to keep the car from driving the engine. Car will slow down (very little load on rear axle gears).

4. Coast: Throttle closed—engine is braking the car (load is on the coast side of the gear set).

Backlash or play in the running gear can be checked by driving the car on a smooth road at 25 mph (40 km./h.) and lightly pressing and releasing the accelerator pedal. Backlash is indicated by a slapping noise with each movement of the accelerator pedal. Raising the car on a lubrication rack will permit you to make a more detailed examination.

REAR AXLE TROUBLESHOOTING CHART

TROUBLES & CAUSES

1. **Noise on acceleration**
   1a. Heavy heel contact on ring gear
2. **Noise on coast**
   2a. Heavy toe contact on ring gear
3. **Noise on both coast and acceleration**
   3a. Differential gears worn
   3b. Pinion and ring gears worn
   3c. Defective bearings

4. **Noise only when rounding a curve**
   4a. Damaged differential case gears
5. **Backlash**
   5a. Worn axle shaft splines
   5b. Loose axle shaft nut
   5c. Worn universal joints
   5d. Excessive play between pinion and ring gear
   5e. Worn differential bearings
   5f. Worn differential side gear thrust washers and/or case
6. **Vibration**
   6a. Worn universal joints
   6b. Universal spline not assembled according to matching arrows
   6c. Undercoating applied to drive shaft
   6d. Drive line center bearing out of alignment
   6e. Drive line angle incorrect

TROUBLESHOOTING THE FRONT END

Drive the car on a smooth road at about 30 mph (48 km./h.), and then take your hands off the steering wheel. The car should maintain a straight course. If the road is crowned, it may cause the car to wander toward the low side of the road and, therefore, it may be necessary to make this test evenly straddled over the center line. Choose a road with no traffic to make this test. On a windy day, the test should be duplicated by going back and forth over the same road. Uneven front-end angles will cause the car to wander to one side.

Hold your hand lightly on the steering wheel at about 30 mph (48 km./h.) to check whether any shocks are being transmitted back to the steering wheel. A constantly jiggling wheel indicates that the front wheels are out of balance. This constant movement is very tiring to a driver on long trips and is hard on every moving part of the front end.

Turn into a deserted side street at about 25 mph (40 km./h.), and then release the steering wheel; it should come back to a straight-ahead position without any assistance from the driver; otherwise, there is binding in the linkage, insufficient caster, or insufficient steering axis inclination.

To check for misalignment, stop the car and inspect the front tires for uneven tread wear. Pass your hand over the surface of each tire tread. Sharp edges felt going one way are called feather edges and are developed from sideward scuffing. Be especially critical of the right-front tire wear, as this wheel is most frequently knocked out of alignment by bumping the curb. When the right-front wheel tire is worn more unevenly than the left, it is an indication of a bent steering arm.

FRONT-END TROUBLESHOOTING CHART

TROUBLES & CAUSES

1. **Excessive looseness**
   1a. Improper adjustment of the steering gear
   1b. Worn steering linkage
   1c. Loose wheel bearing adjustment on worm bearings
   1d. Worn king pins or ball joints

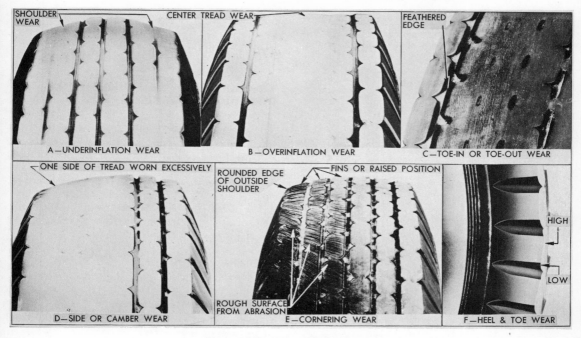

Types of tire wear and their causes.

1e. Loose steering gear mounting
2. **Hard steering**
   2a. Tight adjustment of the steering gear
   2b. Lubrication needed
   2c. Low tire pressure
   2d. Wheels out of alignment
   2e. Excessive caster
3. **Wanders**
   3a. Loose front wheel bearings
   3b. Loose steering linkage
   3c. Loose front end supports
   3d. Uneven tire pressure
   3e. Low pressure in both rear tires
   3f. Incorrect caster
   3g. Bent spindle arm
   3h. Sagging spring
4. **Pulls to one side**
   4a. Uneven caster
   4b. Uneven camber
   4c. Uneven tire pressure
   4d. Frame out of alignment
   4e. Tire sizes not uniform
   4f. Bent spindle arm
   4g. Sagging spring
5. **Shimmy, low speed**
   5a. Loose support arms
   5b. Loose linkage
   5c. Loose wheel bearings
   5d. Soft springs
   5e. Static unbalance of front wheels
   5f. Incorrect tire pressure
6. **Shimmy, high speed**
   6a. Dynamic unbalance of front wheels
   6b. Too much caster
   6c. Soft springs
7. **Squeals on turns**
   7a. Low tire pressure
   7b. Incorrect camber

7c. Bent spindle arm
7d. Frame out of alignment
8. **Excessive tire wear**
   8a. Improper toe-in
   8b. Improper turning radius
   8c. Underinflation
   8d. Overinflation
   8e. Grabbing
   8f. Excessive camber

TROUBLESHOOTING A HYDRAULIC BRAKE SYSTEM

Perhaps the most common complaint about brakes is that the car cannot be brought to a satisfactory stop. As the lining wears, the brake pedal must be pushed down farther and farther in order to move the brake shoes into contact with the drums. Eventually, it reaches the floorboard, and an emergency application does not stop the car. When this happens, it is necessary to adjust the position of the brake shoes so that they are closer to the drums. This restores the pedal to its former position.

Generally, a soft pedal, or one that goes slowly to the floorboard under continued pressure, is caused by air trapped in the hydraulic lines or by a leak in the system. The system must be bled to get rid of the air. To repair the leak, the defective unit must be removed. However, it is considered good practice to overhaul the entire hydraulic system in the event of a leak in any one part, because all of the units are in the same condition; unless repaired at the same time, they too will soon leak.

Another frequent complaint has to do with noise. Actually, the squeals and squeaks that are heard are due to loose parts, which cause high-frequency vibration.

HYDRAULIC BRAKE SYSTEM TROUBLESHOOTING CHART

TROUBLES & CAUSES

1. **Pedal goes to floorboard**
   1a. Brake shoes out of adjustment
   1b. Brake fluid level low
   1c. Leaking lines or cylinders
   1d. Air in brake lines
   1e. Defective master cylinder
2. **One brake drags**
   2a. Incorrect shoe adjustment
   2b. Clogged brake line
   2c. Sluggish wheel cylinder piston
   2d. Weak brake shoe return spring
   2e. Loose wheel bearing
   2f. Brake shoe binding on backing plate
   2g. Out-of-round drum
3. **All brakes drag**
   3a. Insufficient play in master cylinder push rod
   3b. Master cylinder relief port plugged
   3c. Lubricating oil in system instead of hydraulic fluid
   3d. Master cylinder piston sticking
4. **Car pulls to one side**
   4a. Brake fluid or grease on lining
   4b. Sluggish wheel cylinder piston
   4c. Weak retracting spring
   4d. Loose wheel bearing
   4e. Wrong brake lining
   4f. Drum out-of-round
5. **Soft pedal**
   5a. Air in system
   5b. Improper anchor adjustment
   5c. Improper linings
   5d. Thin drums
   5e. Warped brake shoes
6. **Hard pedal**
   6a. Wrong brake lining
   6b. Glazed brake lining
   6c. Mechanical resistance at pedal or shoes
7. **One or more wheels grab**
   7a. Grease or hydraulic fluid on lining
   7b. Loose wheel bearings
   7c. Loose front end supports
   7d. Loose backing plate
   7e. Distorted brake shoe
   7f. Improper brake lining
   7g. Primary and secondary shoes reversed
8. **Erratic braking action**
   8a. Loose brake support
   8b. Loose front end suspension parts
   8c. Grease or hydraulic fluid on lining
   8d. Binding of the shoes in the guides
   8e. Sticking hydraulic wheel cylinder piston
9. **Noisy brakes**
   9a. Loose backing plate
   9b. Loose wheel bearing adjustment
   9c. Loose front end supports
   9d. Warped brake shoes
   9e. Linings loose on shoes
   9f. Improperly installed brake shoes

   9g. Improper anchor adjustment
   9h. Loose brake shoe guides
   9i. Weak brake return springs
   9j. Dust in rivet holes
   9k. Grease or hydraulic fluid on brake lining

TROUBLESHOOTING THE CALIPER DISC BRAKE SYSTEM

Disc brakes are generally mounted on the front wheels, and non-servo, drum-type brakes are mounted on the rear. On other installations, all four wheels have disc brakes. The brakes are frequently actuated by a power unit on the larger cars.

The usual hydraulic brake troubleshooting procedures apply with the following Troubleshooting Chart showing specific complaints:

CALIPER DISC BRAKE TROUBLE-SHOOTING CHART

TROUBLES & CAUSES

1. **Brake pedal meets no resistance; brake pedal has soft or spongy feel**
   1a. Insufficient brake fluid in reservoir
   1b. Air in brake system
2. **Brake pedal can be depressed without braking effect, after bleeding**
   2a. Leaky brake lines
3. **Brake pedal can be depressed after extensive downhill driving (soft and spongy)**
   3a. Inferior or low boiling point fluid, with overheated brake system
   3b. Air in system
4. **Brakes heat up during driving and fail to release**
   4a. Compensating port in master brake cylinder blocked
   4b. Power unit push rod incorrectly adjusted so that master cylinder piston is not released.
   4c. Piston of wheel cylinder sticking
5. **Poor braking effect in spite of high pedal pressure**
   5a. Oil or grease on friction pads
   5b. Glazed friction pads
6. **Brakes pull to one side**
   6a. Brake fluid, oil, or grease on friction pads of one wheel
   6b. Excessive wear of one brake caliper friction pad
   6c. Calipers not parallel to brake disc
7. **Brakes chatter**
   7a. Excessive lateral runout of brake disc
   7b. Bad contact pattern of friction pads
   7c. Rough surface on brake disc
8. **Frequent replenishing of brake fluid in reservoir needed**
   8a. Brake line system leaks
   8b. Master cylinder leaks
   8c. Wheel cylinder leaks
9. **Leaky wheel cylinder**
   9a. Leaking piston seal
   9b. Cylinder walls scored or pitted
   9c. Rust formation on cylinder wall

2

Tuning and Identification

Austin A 40, 1948–59.

Austin-Healey Sprite, 1958–61.

Austin A 55, 1957–61.

Austin-Healey Sprite, Mk II and Mk III, 1962–65.

Austin A 60, 1962–65.

Innocenti Sprite, 1964–65.

Austin 850, 1960–65.

Austin-Healey BN6, BN7, & BT7, 1957–61.

Austin-Healey Mk II BJ7 and Mk III BJ8, 1962–65.

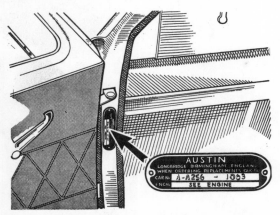

The identification plate is secured to the front door pillar and to the engine compartment firewall.

GENERAL INFORMATION—BMC CARS

IDENTIFICATION

A code is used on chassis and engine numbers for model identification on all BMC cars. The chassis number is stamped on a plate secured to the front door pillar, while the engine number is located on the right-hand side of the cylinder block, above the oil filter.

The car numbering symbol consists of three letters and one figure, followed by the letter (L) if the vehicle has a left-hand drive, and then by the serial number of the car. The first letter designates the make of vehicle, the second the engine capacity, and the third letter the body type. The first figure indicates the series of the model.

FIRST PREFIX LETTER—NAME OF CAR

A—Austin	M—Morris
G—M.G.	R—Riley
H—Healey	W—Wolseley

SECOND PREFIX LETTER—CAPACITY

A—800–999 cc	G—1,000–1,399 cc
B—2,000–2,999 cc	H—1,400–1,999 cc
D—3,000–3,999 cc	L—Up to 799 cc

THIRD PREFIX LETTER—BODY TYPE

A—Ambulance	C—Chassis
D—Coupe	H—Hearse
J—Convertible	K—Truck
N—2-seat Tourer	P—Hard top
S—4-door Saloon	2S—2-door Saloon
T—4-seat Tourer	U—Pickup
V—Van	W—Taxi

FOURTH PREFIX

Series of a model; used to record a major change.

FIFTH PREFIX

L—Left-hand drive

ENGINE IDENTIFICATION

The engine number is composed of a series of letters and numbers to indicate the capacity, make, and type of power unit, the accessories and compression ratio, together with the serial number of the engine.

FIRST PREFIX NUMBER—CAPACITY

8—803 cc	9—950 cc
12—1,200 cc	15—1,500 cc
16—1,600 cc	22—2,200 cc
25—2,500 cc	26—2,600 cc
	29—2,900 cc

FIRST PREFIX LETTER—CAR MAKE

A—Austin	G—M.G.
D—Austin-Healey	M—Morris
J—Commercial	W—Wolseley
R—Riley	

SECOND PREFIX GROUP—TRANSMISSION AND AUXILIARY EQUIPMENT

A—Automatic transmission
N—Steering column shift lever
P—Police specifications
M—Manumatic clutch
O—Borg Warner overdrive
R—Laycock de Normanville overdrive

THIRD PREFIX GROUP—COMPRESSION AND SERIAL NUMBER

H—High compression   L—Low compression

CODE EXAMPLE

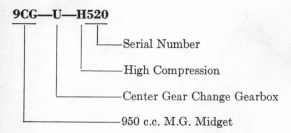

9CG—U—H520
— Serial Number
— High Compression
— Center Gear Change Gearbox
— 950 c.c. M.G. Midget

RECONDITIONED ENGINES

On reconditioned engines the bore and crankshaft sizes are indicated by code letters appearing either under or after the engine number. The bore size is indicated by the first letter and the crankshaft size by the second letter.

The code is as follows:

Code	Bore Oversize	Crankshaft Undersize
A	Standard	Standard
B		0.010 in. (0.254 mm.)
C		0.015 in. (0.381 mm.)
D	0.020 in. (0.508 mm.)	0.020 in. (0.508 mm.)
E		0.025 in. (0.635 mm.)
F	0.030 in. (0.762 mm.)	0.030 in. (0.762 mm.)
G		0.035 in. (0.889 mm.)
H	0.040 in. (1.016 mm.)	0.040 in. (1.016 mm.)
J		0.045 in. (1.143 mm.)
K		0.050 in. (1.270 mm.)
L		0.055 in. (1.397 mm.)
M	0.060 in. (1.524 mm.)	0.060 in. (1.524 mm.)

Thus, engine number 29D/RU/H.12345 M.E. would indicate a reconditioned engine having a cylinder bore 0.060 in. oversize and a crankshaft 0.025 in. undersize.

Reconditioned engines may also be fitted with 0.010 in. oversize valve guides and can be identified by "VG%0.010" stamped on the outside of the cylinder head.

The oversize guides are identified by a shallow groove around their outer diameter.

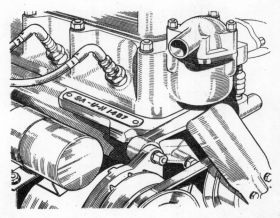

The engine number is stamped on a pad just under No. 1 spark plug.

IGNITION SERVICE NOTES—SPRITE

DISTRIBUTOR DRIVE GEAR

The gear is pinned to an intermediate shaft, and the distributor is driven by an offset coupling.

IGNITION TIMING

The basic timing is 5° BTDC which corresponds to the second pointer on the timing indicator. To adjust the position of the distributor, turn the engine until No. 1 piston is at TDC, firing position. The notch in the pulley will line up with the long pointer on the timing indicator. Turn the engine back about a quarter turn, and then bring it forward again until the notch lines up with the middle arrow on the indicator (5° BTDC). Adjust the distributor position so that the ignition points are just opening.

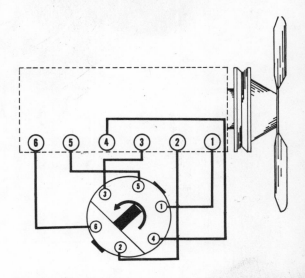

Ignition wiring diagram, Austin-Healey 3,000, Mk II and Mk III.

COMMONLY USED SPECIFICATIONS—AUSTIN, AUSTIN-HEALEY

MODEL		SPARK PLUGS			DISTRIBUTOR			TIMING (Degrees) B = Before Top Dead Center	VALVE CLEARANCE		ENGINE IDLING SPEED (Rpm)	FRONT END ALIGNMENT			
		Make and Type	Gap		Point gap		Cam angle (Degrees)		Int. & Exh. C—Cold H—Hot			Caster (Degrees) P = Positive	Camber (Degrees) N = Negative	Toe-in	
			In.	Mm.	In.	Mm.			In.	Mm.				In.	Mm.
AUSTIN:															
A40	LC	ChN5	.025	.635	.015	.381	45	2B	.012C	.305C	800	P3	P1	1/16-1/8	1.59-3.18
	HC	ChN5	.025	.635	.015	.381	45	5B	.012C	.305C	800	P3	P1	1/16-1/8	1.59-3.18
A55	LC	ChN8	.025	.635	.015	.381	49	TDC	.012H	.305H	800	P1½	P1	0-1/8	0-3.18
	HC		.025	.635	.015	.381	49	5B	.012H	.305H	800	P1½	P1	0-1/8	0-3.18
A55 Mk II		ChN5	.025	.635	.015	.381	60	5B	.012H	.305H	800	P3	P¾	Nil	Nil
A60		ChN5	.025	.635	.015	.381	60	4B	.015H	.380H	800	P1½	P¾	1/16-1/8	1.59-3.18
850		ChN5	.025	.635	.015	.381	60	TDC	.012C	.305C	850	P3	P1	1/16	1.59
AUSTIN-HEALEY:															
BN1, BN2		ChN8	.025	.635	.015	.381	38	6B	.012C	.305C	600	P2	P1	1/16-1/8	1.59-3.18
BN4, BN6		ChN5	.025	.635	.015	.381	38	6B	.012C	.305C	600	P2	P1	1/16-1/8	1.59-3.18
BN7, BT7		ChUN12Y ①	.025	.635	.015	.381	35	5B	.012C②	.305C②	600	P2	P1	1/16-1/8	1.59-3.18
BJ7 Mk II		ChUN12Y ①	.025	.635	.015	.381	35	10B④	.012C②	.305C②	600	P2	P1	1/16-1/8	1.59-3.18
BJ8 Mk III		ChUN12Y ①	.025	.635	.015	.381	35	10B④	.012C②	.305C②	600	P2	P1	1/16-1/8	1.59-3.18

COMMONLY USED SPECIFICATIONS—AUSTIN, AUSTIN-HEALEY

MODEL	SPARK PLUGS			DISTRIBUTOR			TIMING (Degrees) B = Before Top Dead Center	VALVE CLEARANCE			ENGINE IDLING SPEED (Rpm)	FRONT END ALIGNMENT				
	Make and Type	Gap		Point gap		Cam angle (Degrees)		Int. & Exh. C—Cold H—Hot				Caster (Degrees) P = Positive	Camber (Degrees) N = Negative	Toe-in		
		In.	Mm.	In.	Mm.			In.	Mm.					In.	Mm.	
AUSTIN:																
Sprite	ChN5	.025	.635	.015	.381	60	5B③	.012H②	.305H②		600	P3	P1	0–⅛	0–3.18	
Sprite Mk II	ChN5	.025	.635	.015	.381	60	5B③	.012H②	.305H②		600	P3	P1	0–⅛	0–3.18	
Sprite Mk III	ChN5	.025	.635	.015	.381	60	5B③	.012H②	.305H②		600	P3	P1	0–⅛	0–3.18	

① Use champion N3 for racing.
② For racing, set valves to 0.015H (0.38 mm. H.).
③ Set timing at 8°B with engine idling at 600 rpm when using a strobe light.
④ Set timing at 15°B with engine idling at 600 rpm when using a strobe light.

Ignition timing marks are located under the crankshaft pulley.

IGNITION SERVICE NOTES— AUSTIN-HEALEY

DISTRIBUTOR DRIVE GEAR

The gear is pinned to the oil pump driveshaft, and an offset coupling drives the distributor shaft.

IGNITION TIMING

The timing should be set to 10° BTDC. Turn the engine until No. 1 piston reaches TDC firing position. The notch in the rear flange of the crankshaft pulley will be in line with the long pointer on the timing chain cover (TDC). Now turn the engine back about a quarter turn, and then bring it up until the mark on the pulley is in line with the first pointer to give the required static setting of 10° BTDC. Connect a 12-volt lamp in parallel with the primary terminal on the distributor, turn on the ignition switch, and move the distributor until the light goes on, which is an indication that the points just opened. Clamp the distributor in this position.

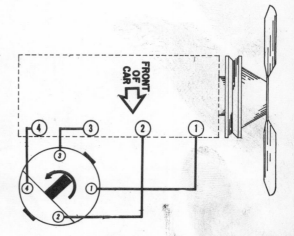

Ignition wiring diagram, Austin 850, 1960–64.

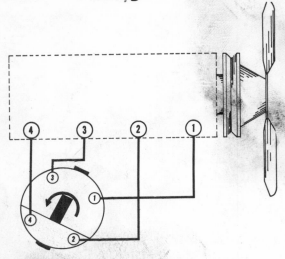

Ignition wiring diagram, Austin-Healey Sprite, 1958–61.

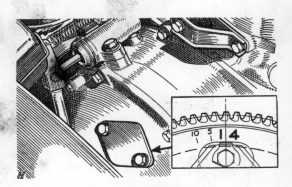

The ignition timing marks for the Austin 850 are visible after removing an inspection plate on the flywheel cover. TDC is indicated by the mark 1/4.

IGNITION SERVICE NOTES—AUSTIN 850

DISTRIBUTOR DRIVE GEAR

The gear is pinned to the oil pump driveshaft, and an offset coupling drives the distributor shaft.

DISTRIBUTOR DRIVE SPINDLE INSTALLATION

Turn the crankshaft until piston No. 1 is at TDC, firing position. Screw a $\frac{5}{16}''$ UNF bolt into the threaded end of the spindle as a handle. Hold it so that the slot is horizontal, with the large offset at the top, and enter it into position. As the gears mesh, the slot will turn counterclockwise until it is approximately at the one o'clock position. Remove the bolt used as a handle.

IGNITION TIMING

The flywheel carries the mark 1/4 to indicate TDC for Nos. 1 and 4 pistons. A 5° and a 10° reference marks are also stamped on the flywheel. These marks are visible with the aid of a mirror after having removed the flywheel inspection cover.

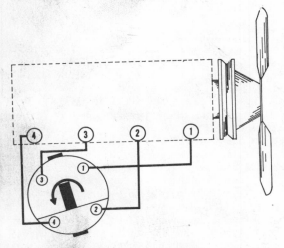

Ignition wiring diagram, Austin-Healey Sprite, Mk II & Mk III, 1962–64.

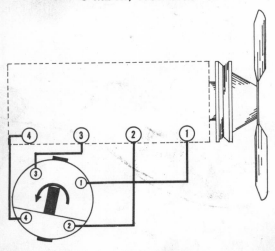

Ignition wiring diagram, Austin A 60.

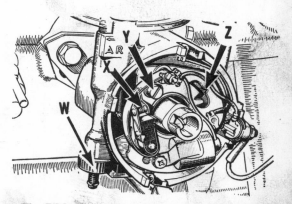

The DM2.P4 distributor exposed to show the contact mechanism, M.G.A. W micrometer adjustment, X contact points, Y lockscrew, and Z slot for adjusting the contact point opening.

GENERAL ENGINE SPECIFICATIONS—AUSTIN, AUSTIN-HEALEY

MODEL	CYL.	BORE		STROKE		DISPLACEMENT		COMPRESSION RATIO	PERFORMANCE	TORQUE	
		In.	Mm.	In.	Mm.	Cu. In.	CC.		SAE (Hp @ Rpm)	(Ft. Lbs. @ Rpm)	(Kg./m. @ Rpm)
AUSTIN:											
A40-A2S6	4	2.478	62.9	3.00	76.2	57.87	948	7.2/1.0	32 @ 4600	48 @ 2200	6.63 @ 2200
								8.3/1.0	34 @ 4800	50 @ 2000	6.91 @ 2000
A40-GS4, GS5	4	2.578	65.5	3.50	88.9	73.17	1200	7.2/1.0	42 @ 4500	58 @ 2400	8.0 @ 2400
A55-HS6, Mk II	4	2.875	73.025	3.50	88.9	90.88	1489	7.2/1.0	47 @ 4100	74 @ 2100	10.3 @ 2100
								8.3/1.0	51 @ 4250	81 @ 2000	11.2 @ 2000
A60	4	3.0	76.2	3.5	88.9	99.08	1622	8.3/1.0	68 @ 5000	89 @ 2500	12.3 @ 2500
850	4	2.478	62.9	2.687	68.26	51.79	848	8.3/1.0	37 @ 5500		
AUSTIN-HEALEY:											
BN1, BN2	6	3.4375	87.3	4.375	111.1	162.2	2660	7.5/1.0	90 @ 4000	150 @ 2000	20.74 @ 2000
BN4, 4-port head	6	3.125	79.375	3.50	88.9	161	2639	8.25/1.0	102 @ 4600	142 @ 2400	19.77 @ 2400
BN6, BN4, 6-port head								8.7/1.0	117 @ 5000	150 @ 3000	20.74 @ 3000
BN7, BT7, 3000 Mk I, 3000 Mk II	6	3.281	83.34	3.50	88.9	177.7	2912	9.0/1.0	124 @ 4600①	167 @ 2700	23.14 @ 2700
BJ8, 3000 Mk III	6	3.281	83.34	3.50	88.9	177.7	2912	9.03/1.0	150 @ 5250	173 @ 3000	23.91 @ 3000
Sprite	4	2.478	62.9	3.00	76.2	57.87	948	8.3/1.0	43 @ 5200	52 @ 3300	7.19 @ 3300
Sprite Mk II	4	2.478	62.9	3.00	76.2	57.87	948	9.1/1.0	48 @ 5400	52 @ 4000	7.19 @ 4000
Sprite Mk II & Mk III	4	2.543	64.58	3.296	83.72	67.0	1098	8.9/1.0	59 @ 5750	62 @ 3250	8.58 @ 3250

① 3000 Mk II was rated at 132 hp @ 4750 rpm.

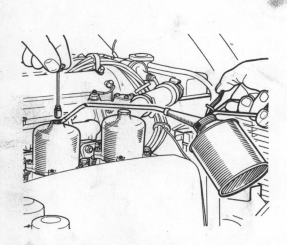

The carburetor has a hydraulic piston damper which must be filled with oil; otherwise, poor acceleration and spitting back will occur. To fill the chamber, unscrew the cap and lift out the damper valve. Fill the hollow piston with oil every 2,500 miles.

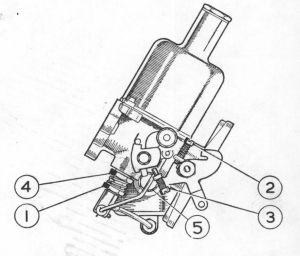

1. Jet adjusting nut.
2. Throttle adjusting screw.
3. Fast-idle adjustment screw.
4. Jet locking nut.
5. Float-chamber bolt.

Carburetor adjusting screws, Sprite.

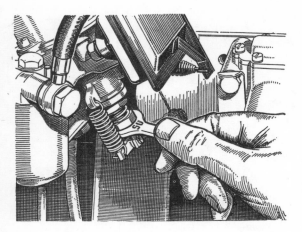

The jet adjusting nut is under the carburetor.

ADJUSTING THE CARBURETOR

Adjusting the mixture of an S.U. carburetor is relatively simple. It is only necessary to adjust the position of the jet up or down along the tapered needle until the air-fuel mixture is correct at idle. As the air throttle is opened, the increased air velocity lifts the piston which, in turn, lifts the tapered needle out of the jet to richen the mixture so as to compensate for the additional air.

Each S.U. carburetor has a piston-lifting pin (*arrow*) for checking the air-fuel ratio. To check the mixture, lift the piston about 1/32" with the lifting pin, or with a screwdriver inserted in the air intake port. The engine should speed up momentarily slightly if the mixture is correctly adjusted. If the engine speed increases and continues to run faster, the mixture is too rich. If the engine speed decreases, the mixture is too lean.

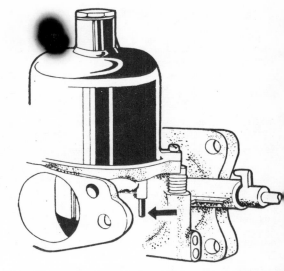

The lifting pin (arrow) is used to test the air-fuel mixture.

Synchronizing the Carburetors

Start the engine and adjust the idle speed to 500 rpm by turning each idle volume screw in an equal amount. Listen to the hiss of the air entering each carburetor in order to equalize the speeds. When the carburetors have been synchronized, turn each idle mixture adjusting screw (out for a leaner mixture and in for a richer mixture) an equal amount until the fastest idle speed is obtained consistent with even firing. It may be necessary to readjust the idle speed by turning down the idle volume screws equal amounts. To check the mixture, lift the piston of each carburetor approximately 1/32". The engine should speed up momentarily slightly if the mixture is correctly adjusted.

The electric fuel pump filter should be cleaned every 6,000 miles (10,000 km.).

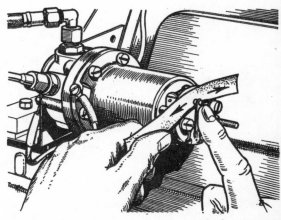

The contact points of the electric fuel pump can be cleaned by drawing a strip of sandpaper between them. Be sure to use a tape with carbon tetrachloride to remove all particles from between the points so that good electrical contact can be made.

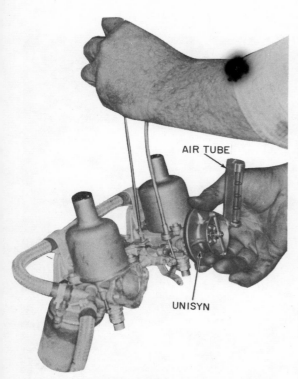

Synchronizing twin carburetors can be done by adjusting the idling speed until each pulls the same vacuum as measured on this Unisyn device.

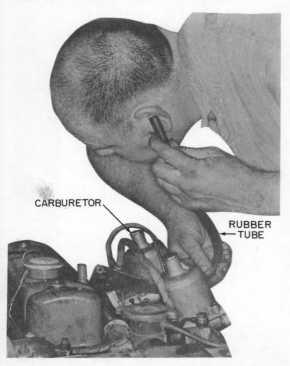

The carburetors can also be synchronized by listening to the air intake noise through a piece of windshield wiper tubing. Adjust until the hiss is equal.

ROAD TESTS

The road tests that are part of this chapter are made by trained drivers of the *Road & Track* magazine staff. Their stated policy in accumulating this data is to tell the reader how the car performs and how well it will fulfill the function for which it is intended.

The speedometer is the first instrument checked because much of the resulting data depends on an accurate speedometer. The speedometer error is determined by making several timed runs over a measured quarter mile course at increments of 10 mph speeds.

The gear ratios are shown in two columns; the figures on the right being those at the rear wheels, and those at the left are the actual box ratios.

The brake test data is gathered by running the car at 80 mph, and then applying the brakes as firmly as possible without locking the wheels. The measurement is made on a decelerometer.

The grade climbing ability of the car is measured with a Tapley meter. The figure shown is the maximum percentage grade that the car can climb in each gear. It is necessary to bear in mind that a 100% grade rises one foot for every foot forward, or is a 45° slope. The Tapley meter can also be used to measure drag, and the procedure is to accelerate to 80 mph on level ground and then coast back down to 60 mph. To ensure accuracy, several runs are made in each direction to compensate for slight changes in grade and wind variations.

The calculated data panel contains useful information not obtainable from the usual measured sources. *The pounds/horsepower* unit is the power-to-weight ratio. The *cubic feet per ton/mile* represents the volume of air pumped by the engine per ton of weight and per mile in high gear. When compared with the same item for other cars, it gives an excellent indication of the performance to be expected in high gear. It is calculated by dividing the displacement in half (because every second down stroke is a working stroke), and then multiplying by the engine revolutions per mile. Then the result is divided by the weight of the car to include the weight factor. *Mph per 1,000 rpm* is closely related to *piston travel in feet per mile*, which shows the number of feet traveled by the piston for each mile. These two figures are an indication of the longevity of the engine because they show the amount of activity in the engine compartment required to propel the car over a given distance.

The R&T wear index is useful in determining the amount of engine wear that can be expected. It is calculated by multiplying the engine rpms/mile by the piston travel, and then dividing by 100,000 to obtain a reasonable figure. While this figure does not take into account differences in engine design or the quality of materials used, the results do seem to be surprisingly accurate as a wear index.

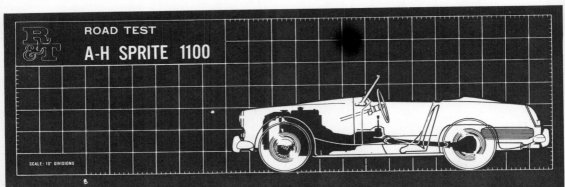

ROAD TEST

A-H SPRITE 1100

SCALE: 10" DIVISIONS

DIMENSIONS

Wheelbase, in	80.5
Tread, f and r	47.2/45.0
Over-all length, in	138
width	54.0
height	47.8
equivalent vol, cu ft	206
Frontal area, sq ft	14.3
Ground clearance, in	6.2
Steering ratio, o/a	n s.
turns, lock to lock	2.3
turning circle, ft	30
Hip room, front	2 x 16
Hip room, rear	n. a.
Pedal to seat back, max.	41.0
Floor to ground	7.2

CALCULATED DATA

Lb/hp (test wt)	34.2
Cu ft/ton mile	80.4
Mph/1000 rpm (4th)	15.4
Engine revs/mile	3900
Piston travel, ft/mile	2140
Rpm @ 2500 ft/min	4550
equivalent mph	70.0
R&T wear index	83.5

SPECIFICATIONS

List price	$1985
Curb weight, lb	1560
Test weight	1880
distribution, %	51/49
Tire size	5.20-13
Brake swept area	190
Engine type	4-cyl, ohv
Bore & stroke	2.54 x 3.30
Displacement, cc	1098
cu in	66.98
Compression ratio	8.90
Bhp @ rpm	55 @ 5500
equivalent mph	84.6
Torque, lb-ft	61 @ 2500
equivalent mph	38.4

GEAR RATIOS

4th (1.000)	4.22
3rd (1.357)	5.73
2nd (1.918)	8.09
1st (3.222)	13.6

SPEEDOMETER ERROR

30 mph	actual, 29.3
60 mph	57.8

PERFORMANCE

Top speed (5530), mph	85
Shifts, rpm-mph	
3rd (6000)	68
2nd (6000)	48
1st (6050)	29

FUEL CONSUMPTION

Normal range, mpg	30/36

ACCELERATION

0-30 mph, sec	5.4
0-40	8.3
0-50	12.5
0-60	18.3
0-70	27.8
0-80	42.5
0-100	
Standing ¼ mile	20.9
speed at end	63

TAPLEY DATA

4th, maximum gradient, %	9.8
3rd	13.5
2nd	19.3
Total drag at 60 mph, lb	75

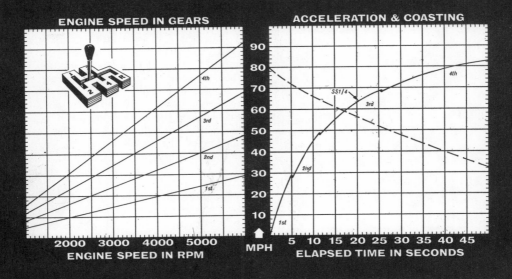

ENGINE SPEED IN GEARS

ENGINE SPEED IN RPM

ACCELERATION & COASTING

ELAPSED TIME IN SECONDS

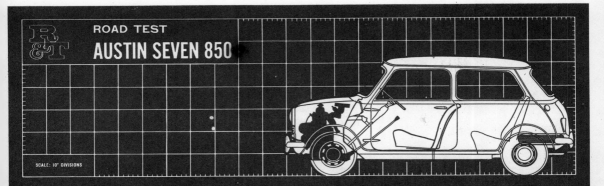

ROAD TEST

AUSTIN SEVEN 850

SCALE: 10" DIVISIONS

DIMENSIONS

Wheelbase, in.........80.0
Tread, f and r.....48.2/46.2
Over-all length, in......120
  width..........55.5
  height.........53.0
  equivalent vol, cu ft....204
Frontal area, sq ft......20.4
Ground clearance, in.....6.0
Steering ratio, o/a........n.a.
  turns, lock to lock......2.3
  turning circle, ft......33
Hip room, front.....2 x 20.0
Hip room, rear......42.0
Pedal to seat back, max..39.0
Floor to ground.........6.0

CALCULATED DATA

Lb/hp (test wt).........44.7
Cu ft/ton mile..........72.5
Mph/1000 rpm (4th)......15.0
Engine revs/mile........4000
Piston travel, ft/mile....1790
Rpm @ 2500 ft/min......5590
  equivalent mph......83.8
R&T wear index........71.6

SPECIFICATIONS

List price.............$1295
Curb weight, lb.......1340
Test weight..........1655
  distribution, %.....61/39
Tire size............5.20-10
Brake swept area.......110
Engine type.....4 cyl, ohv
Bore & stroke....2.48 x 2.69
Displacement, cc.......848
  cu in............51.7
Compression ratio.......8.3
Bhp @ rpm.....37 @ 5500
  equivalent mph....82.5
Torque, lb-ft....44 @ 2900
  equivalent mph....43.5

GEAR RATIOS

4th (1.00)..........3.77
3rd (1.41).........5.32
2nd (2.17).........8.18
1st (3.62).........13.7

SPEEDOMETER ERROR

30 mph.........actual, 28.1
60 mph..............57.4

PERFORMANCE

Top speed (mfr), mph.....75
  best timed run.....70.0
  3rd (5800)..........62
  2nd (5800)..........40
  1st (5800)..........23

FUEL CONSUMPTION

Normal range, mpg.....28/36

ACCELERATION

0-30 mph, sec..........6.5
0-40.................11.5
0-50.................18.7
0-60.................29.6
0-70.................
0-80.................
0-100................
Standing ¼ mile.......23.6
  speed at end..........55

TAPLEY DATA

4th, lb/ton @ mph..170 @ 37
3rd.............245 @ 28
2nd.............360 @ 23
Total drag at 60 mph, lb...95

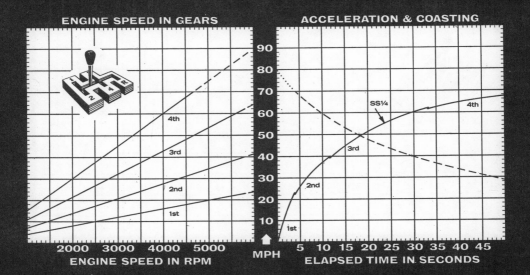

ENGINE SPEED IN GEARS

4th
3rd
2nd
1st

2000 3000 4000 5000
ENGINE SPEED IN RPM

ACCELERATION & COASTING

90
80
70
60
50
40
30
20
10
MPH

SS¼
4th
3rd
2nd
1st

5 10 15 20 25 30 35 40 45
ELAPSED TIME IN SECONDS

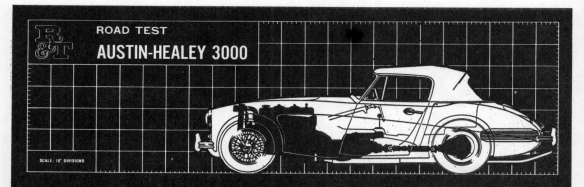

ROAD TEST

AUSTIN-HEALEY 3000

SCALE: 10" DIVISIONS

DIMENSIONS

Wheelbase, in	92.0
Tread, f and r	48.7/50.0
Over-all length, in	157.5
width	60.5
height	50.0
equivalent vol, cu ft	274
Frontal area, sq ft	16.8
Ground clearance, in	4.5
Steering ratio, o/a	n.a.
turns, lock to lock	2.5
turning circle, ft	35
Hip room, front	2 x 18.0
Hip room, rear	36.0
Pedal to seat back	43.0
Floor to ground	9.0

CALCULATED DATA

Lb/hp (test wt)	20.3
Cu ft/ton mile	94.5
Mph/1000 rpm (o/d)	23.7
Engine revs/mile	2535
Piston travel, ft/mile	1480
Rpm @ 2500 ft/min	4290
equivalent mph	101
R&T wear index	37.5

SPECIFICATIONS

List price	n.a.
Curb weight, lb	2430
Test weight	2760
distribution, %	48/52
Tire size	5.90-15
Brake swept area	n.a.
Engine type	6-cyl, ohv
Bore & stroke	3.28 x 3.50
Displacement, cc	2912
cu in	177.7
Compression ratio	9.03
Bhp @ rpm	136 @ 4750
equivalent mph	112
Torque, lb-ft	167 @ 3000
equivalent mph	71

GEAR RATIOS

o/d (0.82)	3.20
4th (1.00)	3.91
3rd (1.31)	5.12
2nd (2.05)	8.02
1st (2.93)	11.5

SPEEDOMETER ERROR

30 mph	actual, 29.2
60 mph	59.4

PERFORMANCE

Top speed (4850), mph	115
best timed run	n.a.
3rd (5200)	77
2nd (5200)	49
1st (5200)	34

FUEL CONSUMPTION

Normal range, mpg	15/21

ACCELERATION

0-30 mph, sec	3.5
0-40	5.5
0-50	8.2
0-60	11.2
0-70	14.7
0-80	19.8
0-100	37.0
Standing ¼ mile	17.6
speed at end	77

TAPLEY DATA

4th, lb/ton @ mph	265 @ 54
3rd	365 @ 48
2nd	540 @ 41
Total drag at 60 mph, lb	120

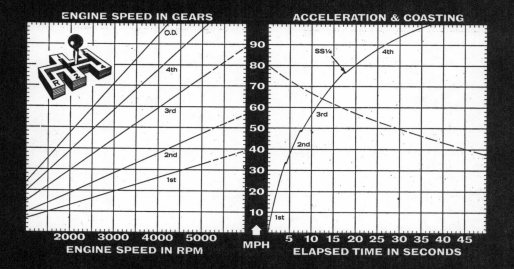

ENGINE SPEED IN GEARS

ACCELERATION & COASTING

O.D.

4th

3rd

2nd

1st

SS¼   4th

3rd

2nd

1st

90 80 70 60 50 40 30 20 10

MPH

2000   3000   4000   5000
ENGINE SPEED IN RPM

5 10 15 20 25 30 35 40 45
ELAPSED TIME IN SECONDS

CAPACITIES—AUSTIN, AUSTIN-HEALEY

MODEL	FUEL TANK			RADIATOR			CRANKCASE			TRANSMISSION			OVERDRIVE			DIFFERENTIAL			TIRE PRESSURE			
	Gallon			Pints			Pints			Pints			Pints			Pints			Front		Rear	
	U.S.	Imp.	Ltr.	U.S.	Imp.	Ltr.	U.S.	Imp.	Ltr.	U.S.	Imp.	Ltr.	U.S.	Imp.	Ltr.	U.S.	Imp.	Ltr.	Psi	Kg./cm.²	Psi	Kg./cm.²
AUSTIN:																						
A40-A2S6	6.9	5.75	26.5	9.6	8.0	4.54	6.6①	5.5	3.12	2.4	2.0	1.14	–	–	–	2.3	1.75	1.0	20	1.4	20	1.4
A40 Countryman	6.9	5.75	26.5	9.6	8.0	4.54	6.6①	5.5	3.12	2.4	2.0	1.14	–	–	–	2.3	1.75	1.0	22	1.6	24	1.7
A55	10.5	8.75	40	14.4	12	6.82	8.4②	7	4	4.8	4	2.3	6.0	5	2.9	2.4	2	1.14	26	1.8	26	1.8
A55 Mk II	12	10	45.4	13.8	11.5	6.5	8.4①	7	4	6	5	2.84	–	–	–	2.4	2	1.14	23	1.6	25	1.75
A60	12	10	45.4	10.8	9	5.1	9②	7.5	4.3	5.4	4.5	2.57	13.5	11.3	6.4	2.75	2.25	1.28	23	1.6	25	1.75
850	6.6	5.5	25	6.3	5.25	3.0	10.8①	8	5.1	–	–	–	–	–	–	–	–	–	24	1.7	22	1.6
AUSTIN-HEALEY:																						
BN1, BN2	14.4	12	54.5	24	20	10.8	14.1②	11.75	6.68	–	–	–	6.6	5.5	3.12	3.6	3	1.7	20	1.4	23	1.6
BN4, BN6	14.4	12	54.5	24	20	10.8	12.3③	10.25	5.85	6	5	2.84	7.5	6.25	3.55	3.6	3	1.7	20	1.4	23	1.6
BN7, BT7, BJ7 & BJ8	14.4	12	54.5	21.6③	18③	10.2③	12.3③	10.25	5.85	6	5	2.84	7.5	6.25	3.55	3.6	3	1.7	20	1.4	23	1.6
Sprite Mk I, II & III	7.2	6	27.3	12	10	5.7	7.8	6.5	3.7	2.7	2.3	1.3	–	–	–	1.8	1.5	.85	18	1.27	20	1.41

① Add 1.2 U.S., 1.0 Imp., 0.57 liter for new filter.
② Add 1.5 U.S., 1.25 Imp., 0.71 liter for new filter.
③ Without heater.

3

The Fuel System

These B.M.C. cars use an S.U. electric fuel pump and an S.U. carburetor. The pump delivers the fuel from the tank to the carburetor, which is an air valve type. The S.U. carburetor contains a single jet in which a tapered needle moves up or down according to the flow of air which, of course, is regulated by the throttle opening. Both the fuel pump and carburetor service procedures will be covered in this chapter.

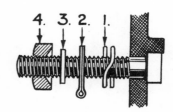

Assembly details for the terminal parts.

ELECTRIC FUEL PUMP SERVICE

To disassemble the pump: 1. Unscrew the filler plug. 2. Remove the inlet and outlet unions. 3. Remove the valve cage, cage washer, valve, and spring. 4. Lift out the wire retaining clip and withdraw the valve disc. 5. Take out the six screws holding the two main parts of the pump together. 6. Check the action of the valves by blowing through the inlet. It should be possible to blow freely but not suck air back through the inlet union. The reverse action should be true for the exhaust. 7. To remove the diaphragm, rotate the whole assembly counterclockwise. *CAUTION: Be careful not to drop the rollers behind the diaphragm.* 8. Remove the contact cover and the nut on the terminal which acts as a seat for the cover. 9. Cut away the lead washer squeezed on the terminal threads below the nut, and push the terminal down a short way so that the tag on the coil end is free. 10. Unscrew the contact blade retaining screw and the two long pedestal screws, and then remove the blade and the pedestal. 11. Push out the rocker hinge pin. *CAUTION: Do not disturb the core of the magnet.*

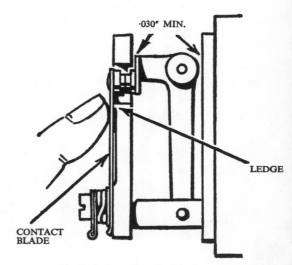

Method of setting the breaker points.

To reassemble the pump: 1. Install each valve with its smooth side facing down and lock it in place with the wire retainer. 2. Install the red fiber washers as follows: the thin one goes below the valve cage, the next thickest one above the cage, and the thickest one on the inlet union. The washer on the filter plug is also a thick red fiber one. 3. Assemble the contact breaker assembly on the pedestal so that the rockers are free but without appreciable sideplay. If the contact blade has been removed, insert it under the tag, and bearing directly against the pedestal. When the points are open, the blade should rest against the ledge of the pedestal, but must not be tight enough to keep the outer rocker from coming forward when the points

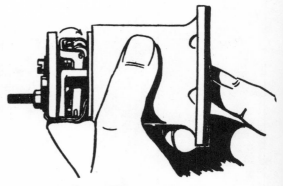

Checking the armature setting.

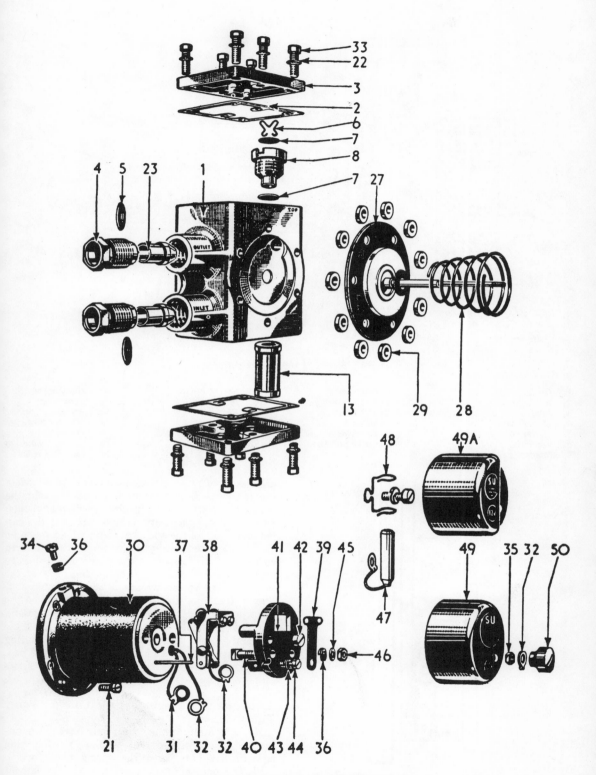

Exploded view of the LCS type pump.

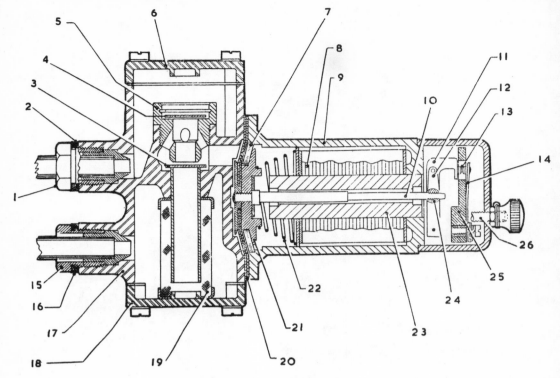

Sectioned view of the LCS type pump.

1. Outlet union.
2. Rubber ring.
3. Inlet valve.
4. Outlet valve.
5. Outlet valve cage.
6. Top cover plate.
7. Spherical rollers.

8. Magnet coil.
9. Iron coil housing.
10. Bronze rod.
11. Outer rocker.
12. Inner rocker.
13. Tungsten points.

14. Spring blade.
15. Inlet union.
16. Rubber ring.
17. Body.
18. Lower cover plate.
19. Filter.

20. Diaphragm.
21. Armature.
22. Armature spring.
23. Magnet core.
24. Trunnion.
25. Bakelite mouldin
26. Terminal screw.

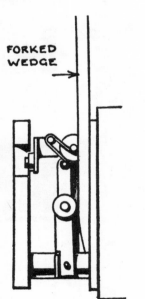

A forked wedge should be used to keep the armature in position when installing the diaphragm.

are closed. The points should make contact when the rocker is at mid-position. To check, hold the blade in contact with the pedestal, without pressing on the overhanging portion, and then test the gap between the rollers and the body, which must be 0.030″. If necessary bend the tip of the blade to correct. *NOTE: Assemble the spring washer on the ground connection screw between the tag and the pedestal.* The spring washer is not a reliable conductor, therefore, the tag must bear directly on the screw head. Solder the coil wires to their tags and the two terminals to the ground wire. Assemble the parts of the terminal screw as follows: spring washer, wiring tag, lead washer, and recessed nut 4. Assemble the armature return spring with its larger end towards the coil.

ADJUSTING THE DIAPHRAGM FOR CONTACT POINT THROW-OVER

If the armature and center rod have been un screwed, it will be necessary to make the following adjustment: (1) Swing the spring blade, which holds the points, to one side. (2) Fit the impact washer into position, and place the 11 guide roller

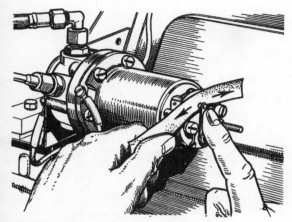

Cleaning the contact points of the pump with sand-paper.

into position around the armature. *CAUTION: Do not use gasket compound on the diaphragm.* (3) Holding the magnet assembly in your left hand in a horizontal position, turn the armature inward until the throw-over mechanism stops operating, and then turn it back a sixth of a turn at a time until the throw-over mechanism just starts to operate, when the armature is pushed in slowly. Now, unscrew the armature an additional two-thirds turn. (4) Place the cast-iron body into position on the main body, taking care to see that the drain hole in the cast-iron body is at the bottom, in line

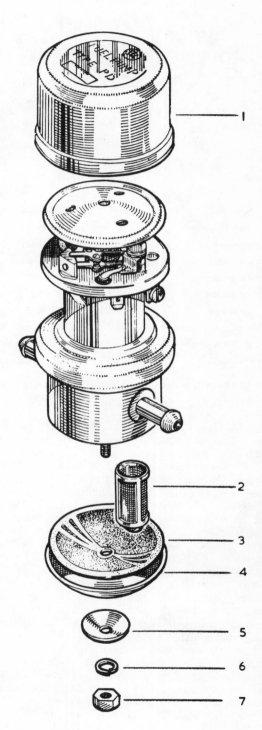

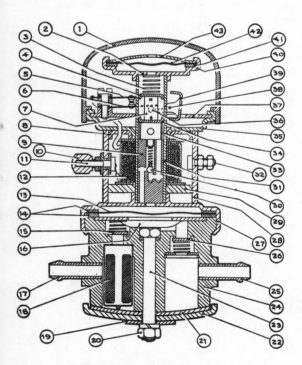

Sectioned view of the PD pump.

Parts of the PD electrical fuel pump.

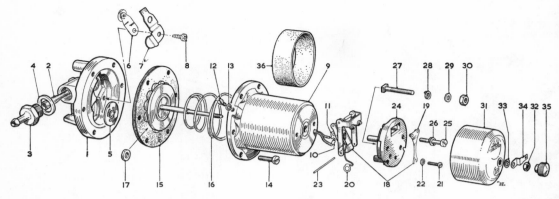

No.	Description	No.	Description	No.	Description
1.	Body.	13.	Washer—spring.	25.	Screw—pedestal to housing.
2.	Filter.	14.	Screw—housing to body.	26.	Washer—spring.
3.	Nozzle inlet.	15.	Diaphragm assembly.	27.	Screw for terminal.
4.	Washer for nozzle.	16.	Spring.	28.	Washer—spring.
5.	Valve—outlet.	17.	Roller.	29.	Washer—lead—for screw.
6.	Valve—inlet.	18.	Rocker and blade.	30.	Nut for screw.
7.	Retainer valve.	19.	Blade.	31.	Cover—end.
8.	Screw for retainer.	20.	Tag—2 B.A. terminal.	32.	Nut for cover.
9.	Housing—coil.	21.	Screw for blade.	33.	Washer—shakeproof.
10.	Tag—5 B.A. terminal.	22.	Washer—dished.	34.	Connector—Lucar.
11.	Tag—2 B.A. terminal.	23.	Spindle for contact breaker.	35.	Knob—terminal.
12.	Screw—earth.	24.	Pedestal.	36.	Sleeve—rubber.

Exploded view of the SP electric fuel pump used since 1963. This pump will not operate unless the terminal voltage is over 10 volts.

with the filter plug in the main body, and that all the rollers are still in their correct positions. *CAUTION: If a roller drops out of position, it will get trapped between the two ports and cut a hole in the diaphragm.* (5) Insert the six body screws. *CAUTION: The diaphragm must be stretched to its outermost position before tightening the screws.* To stretch the diaphragm, insert a matchstick behind one of the white fiber rollers on the outer rocker to hold the contact points together, after first repositioning the spring blade into its normal position. *NOTE: A special forked wedge is available to keep the armature in the correct position.* Now pass current through the pump to energize the magnet, which will pull the armature and the diaphragm forward. Tighten the body screws while in this position.

The following three points are repeated for emphasis: (1) The contact breaker blade must be out of contact while setting the diaphragm; (2) test the armature action by pressing firmly and steadily rather than jerking it while making the adjustment; and (3) make sure you stretch the diaphragm to its limit before tightening the body screws.

S. U. CARBURETORS

This commonly used carburetor is an air-valve type, simple in construction, and relatively trouble-free in operation. An air valve piston moves a tapered needle in or out of a metering jet to provide the correct mixture, depending on the amount of air entering the carburetor. The throttle plate position determines the air velocity, which in turn determines the position of the air valve piston—and also the metering needle. No choke is used, but some models have a solenoid-actuated valve which is opened during cold starts to let additional fuel enter the intake manifold.

OVERHAULING AN S. U. CARBURETOR

DISASSEMBLING
① Remove the cap nut and fuel line assembly. The float chamber cover (A) can now be lifted off and the float removed.

② Turn the carburetor over and remove the cap and the main jet assembly (B). There are a number of ways in which this main jet and its cover are assembled. In some cases, levers are

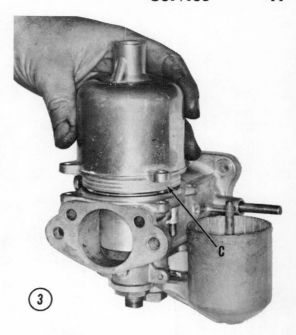

attached to provide a means for moving the jet to correspond to throttle opening and, in some cases, the main jet is attached to a diaphragm to provide a flexible means of making this adjustment.

③ Remove the three screws holding the suction chamber cover, lift off the cover, and remove the piston and spring assembly (C).

CLEANING AND INSPECTING

Clean all parts in carburetor cleaner. Follow

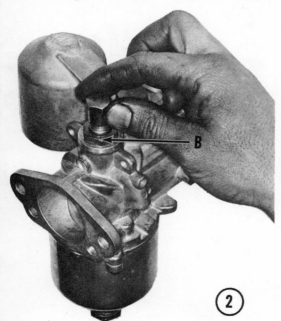

with a solvent bath and blow dry. Diaphragms and parts containing leather should be cleaned only in solvent—never in a carburetor cleaner. Blow compressed air through all passageways and jets to make sure that they are open.

Move the throttle shaft back and forth to check for wear. These carburetors are not sensitive to throttle shaft wear, but, if it is excessive, the shaft can be replaced. In some cases, cork packing glands are provided at each end. These can be replaced to minimize air leaks.

Shake the float to check for a leak. Replace the float if it has liquid in it. Check the float needle lever for a flat spot which indicates replacement to be necessary.

If the main jet was not centered, the jet needle will be worn on one side because of contact with the main jet. In such a case, replace both the needle and the jet. Check the specifications in this chapter for the correct needle, jet, and spring for the model on which you are working. Replace the suction piston spring if rust spots appear anywhere on it. This spring is color coded on the top coil.

Always replace the type of jet assembly which has a diaphragm secured to it, as the diaphragm always leaks if reused.

ASSEMBLING

④ Parts of the main jet are laid out in the order of assembly. The cork sealing ring is assembled over the seating gland nut (D), which holds the assembly in the carburetor. The jet bottom bearing (H) must be friction loaded by means of one or more brass shims (I), as shown in Step ⑤. The mixture adjusting screw (F) moves the jet (G) up or down within the jet top bearing (M).

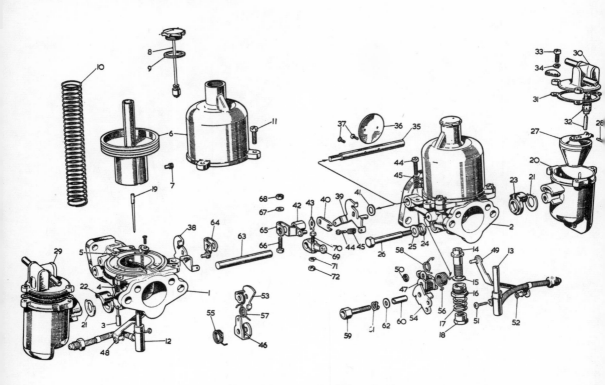

Exploded view of the S.U. carburetor.

⑤ Before making up the main jet assembly, it is important to check the number of shims (I) needed to provide an interference fit for the jet bottom bearing (H). Add one or more shims as required to bring the top edge of the bearing (H) slightly above the rim of the seating gland nut (D).

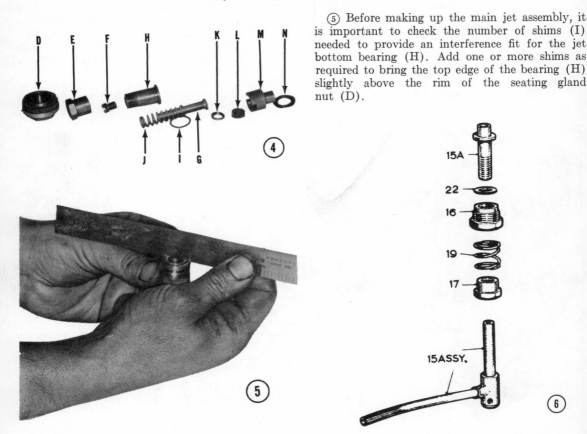

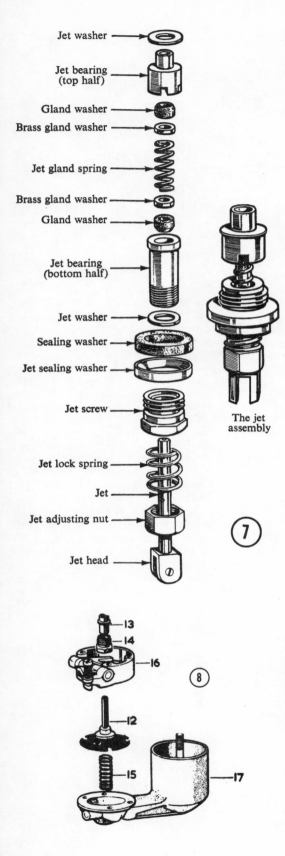

Jet washer

Jet bearing (top half)

Gland washer

Brass gland washer

Jet gland spring

Brass gland washer

Gland washer

Jet bearing (bottom half)

Jet washer

Sealing washer

Jet sealing washer

Jet screw

Jet lock spring

Jet

Jet adjusting nut

Jet head

⑦

The jet assembly

⑨

⑥ On some late-model carburetors, a nylon tube feeds the main jet (15 assy.) from the float chamber. The jet parts are assembled in this manner.

⑦ Some main jets are designed to move with throttle opening. This exploded view shows the details of such an assembly.

⑧ Some main jets are fed fuel from the float chamber (17) through a diaphragm and jet assembly (12) as shown. This flexible mounting allows the cam in the jet unit housing (16) to move the jet and diaphragm assembly (12) up or down, according to throttle movement. The jet bearing (13) and the jet bearing nut (14) keep the jet centralized.

⑨ Install the assembled parts of the main jet into the carburetor body.

⑩ The main jet must be centralized in order to prevent the tapered needle from making contact with it, which would cause sticking and wear. This view shows the main jet improperly positioned off center. Without a proper centralizing tool, the main jet can be approximately centralized by tapping the bottom bearing (H) with a plastic mallet until it is in the center of the casting hole.

13

14

16

⑧

12

15

17

MAIN JET

UNEVEN SPACE

⑩

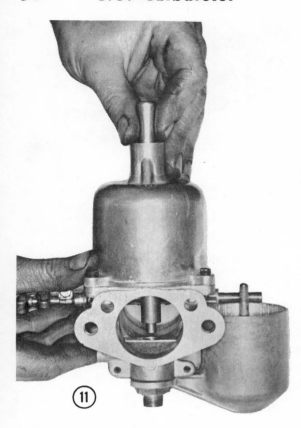

(11)

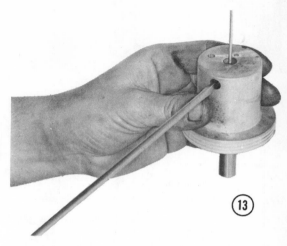

(13)

(11) A centralizing tool is necessary to do this job accurately. To use such a tool, assemble the cover, without the piston, and slide the tool into the main jet. Move the jet while sliding the tool up and down. When the jet is accurately centered, the tool will enter smoothly. Tighten the packing gland firmly at this point.

(12) Install the adjusting screw (O), and then tighten the cap.

(13) Install the needle if a new one is to be used. The shoulder of the needle must be flush with the under face of the piston.

(14) Two types of needles were used on these carburetors, and the correct reference point for each type is indicated by the shoulder line.

(15) Insert the piston and needle assembly. *WARNING: Be careful not to bend the needle during this operation.* A check should be made at this time to be sure that the jet is properly centralized. Install the piston cover without the spring or dashpot assembly. Lift the piston with your finger and let it drop. The jet is centered correctly when the piston falls freely and hits the jet bridge with a sharp metallic click.

(16) Centralizing can be accomplished by raising the jet onto the needle if no tool is available to do the job accurately. To centralize the jet in this manner, loosen the jet locking nut about 1/12 turn and push up the jet as high as possible while gently pressing down on the piston assembly. The process will be facilitated if one side of the carburetor body is tapped lightly with a plastic ham-

O

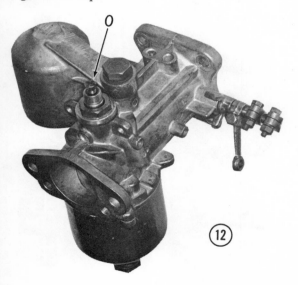

(12)

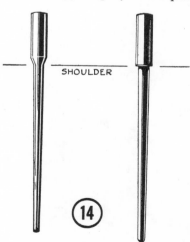

SHOULDER

(14)

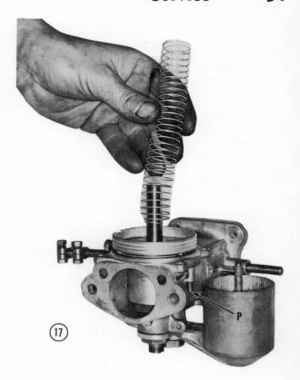

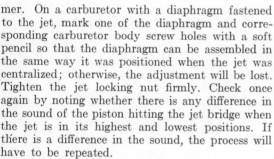

mer. On a carburetor with a diaphragm fastened
to the jet, mark one of the diaphragm and corre-
sponding carburetor body screw holes with a soft
pencil so that the diaphragm can be assembled in
the same way it was positioned when the jet was
centralized; otherwise, the adjustment will be lost.
Tighten the jet locking nut firmly. Check once
again by noting whether there is any difference in
the sound of the piston hitting the jet bridge when
the jet is in its highest and lowest positions. If
there is a difference in the sound, the process will
have to be repeated.

⑰ Lubricate the piston rod with light engine
oil, and then position the spring over it. These
springs are color coded and should be checked
against the specifications in this chapter. The
arrow (P) points out the piston lifting pin which
is used to test the fuel-air mixture when making
the carburetor adjustment.

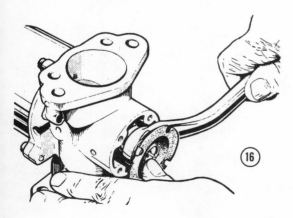

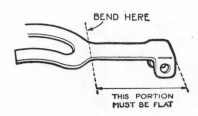

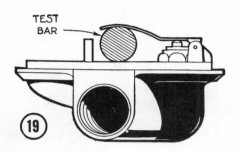

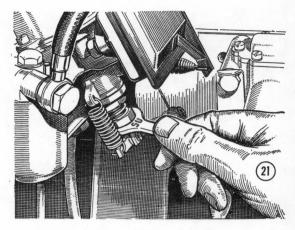

(19) Install a new needle and seat assembly and adjust the float level according to specifications by inserting the correct sized bar under the float lever. Bend at the point indicated.

(20) Insert the float assembly, and then install the cover. Replace the screen and fuel line.

(18) Fill the damper well with light engine oil, and then install the damper assembly. The damper smoothes out fluctuations of the air valve piston which, unless damped, cause leaning of the mixture during acceleration and the development of a flat spot. The well should be filled with light engine oil at each lubrication period and when doing an engine tune up.

Adjusting the Carburetor

(21) Adjusting the mixture of an S.U. carburetor is relatively simple. It is only necessary to adjust the position of the jet up or down along the tapered needle until the fuel-air mixture is correct at idle. As the air throttle is opened, the increased air velocity lifts the piston which, in turn, lifts the tapered needle out of the jet to richen the

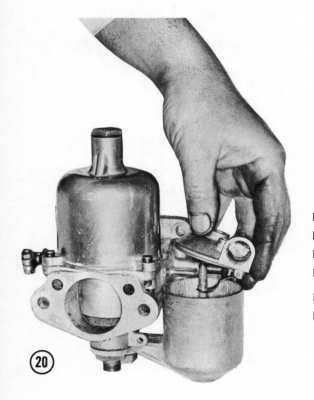

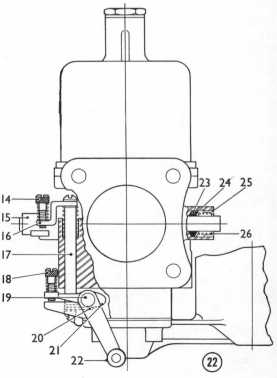

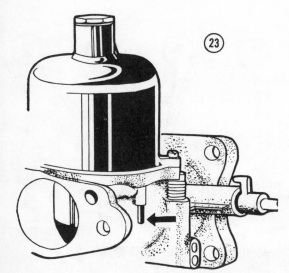

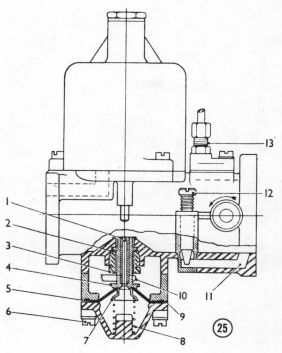

mixture so as to compensate for the additional air. Needles with various tapers are used to compensate for the different sizes of engines. There are two different types of carburetors requiring different adjustments. In this illustration, a wrench is used to screw the adjusting nut up which moves the jet up, thus leaning out the mixture.

㉒ On the diaphragm type of carburetor, the adjustment is made by turning in the jet adjusting screw (18) which is an adjustable stop for the lever controlling the position of the jet. Turning the screw clockwise enriches the fuel-air mixture. The adjustment, like the older models, is made with the engine idling. Adjustment screw (14) is for the purpose of adjusting the idle speed, as it controls the throttle opening.

㉓ Each S. U. carburetor is fitted with a piston lifting pin (*arrow*) for checking the fuel-air ratio. To check the mixture, lift the piston about 1/32" with the lifting pin, or with a screwdriver inserted in the air intake port. The engine should speed up momentarily slightly if the mixture is correctly adjusted. If the engine speed increases and continues to run faster, the mixture is too rich. If the engine speed decreases, the mixture is too lean.

㉔ To adjust the idle speed on nondiaphragm-

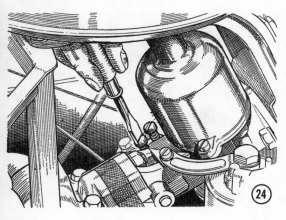

type carburetors, a throttle adjusting screw is provided. Turning the screw in increases engine speed.

㉕ On diaphragm-type carburetors, the idle mixture is adjusted at the main jet (1) and the amount of the mixture passing the closed throttle plate is adjusted by the idle mixture adjusting screw (12). Turning this screw clockwise lessens the amount of fuel-air mixture bypassing the closed throttle (through passageway 11) and thus decreases engine speed.

Synchronizing Twin and Triple Carburetor Installations

㉖ After the engine has been tuned, the carburetors must be synchronized. To do this loosen each bolt which holds a throttle operating lever to the common shaft. Close each throttle valve fully by rotating the throttle shaft clockwise (from the front of the car), and then tighten the clamp bolt. Operate the linkage to see if all throttles are opening simultaneously by noting the movement of the full-throttle stops at the left-hand side of the throttle shafts. For an initial adjustment, turn the idle volume adjustment screws onto their seats lightly, and then back them off two full turns. Turn the mixture adjusting screws 2½ turns down.

㉗ Start the engine and adjust the idle speed to 500 rpm by turning each idle volume screw in an equal amount. Listen to the hiss of the air entering each carburetor in order to equalize the speeds. When the carburetors have been synchronized, turn each mixture adjusting screw (out for a leaner mixture and in for a richer mixture)

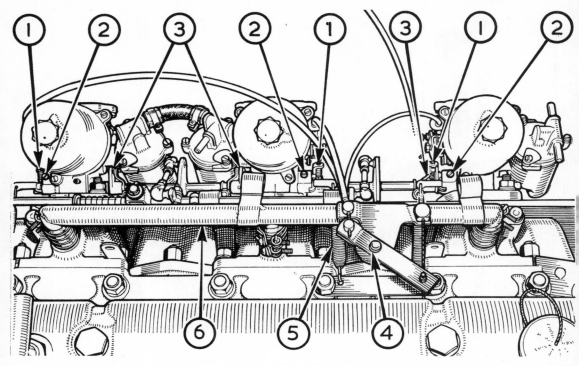

1. Fast idling adjusting screws.
2. Throttle adjusting screws.
3. Throttle operating levers.
4. Choke cable relay lever.
5. Throttle return spring.
6. Balance tube.

(26)

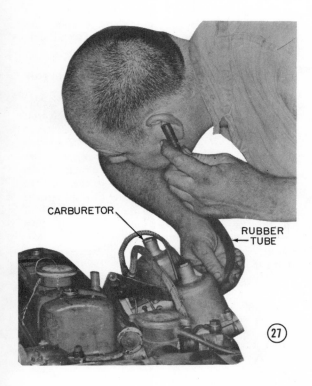

CARBURETOR

RUBBER
← TUBE

(27)

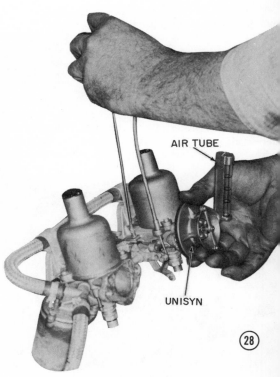

AIR TUBE

UNISYN

(28)

S.U. CARBURETOR SPECIFICATIONS—AUSTIN, AUSTIN-HEALEY

CAR MODEL	CARBURETOR MODEL		FLOAT LEVEL		JET SIZE		NEEDLE TYPE	AIR VALVE SPRING
	Code	Size	In.	Mm.	In.	Mm.		
AUSTIN:								
A55	HS2	1¼	5⁄16	8	.090	2.29	M	
850	HS2	1¼	5⁄16	8	.090	2.29	EB	Red
AUSTIN-HEALEY:								
BN1, BN2	H4(2)	1½	7⁄16	11	.090	2.29	QW	Yellow
BN4, 4-Port head	H4(2)	1½	7⁄16	11	.090	2.29	AJ	Red
BN6, BN4, 6-Port head	HD6(2)	1¾	7⁄16	11	.100	2.54	CV	Yellow
BN7, BT7, 3000 Mk I	HD6(2)	1¾	7⁄16	11	.100	2.54	CV	Green
BN7, BT7, 3000 Mk II	HS4(3)		7⁄16	11	.090	2.29	DJ	Red
BJ7	HS6(2)		7⁄16	11	.100	2.54	BC	
BJ8, Mk III	HD8(3)		1⁄8	3.2	.125	3.18	UH	
Sprite 948cc	HI		5⁄16	8	.090	2.29	GG	
Sprite Mk II 948cc	HS2	1¼	5⁄16	8	.090	2.29	V3	
Sprite Mk II 1098cc							GY	Blue
Sprite Mk III 1098cc							AN	

an equal amount until the fastest idle speed is obtained consistent with even firing. It may be necessary to readjust the idle speed by turning down the idle volume screws equal amounts. To check the mixture, lift the piston of each carburetor approximately ⅓₂". The engine should speed up momentarily slightly if the mixture is correctly adjusted. If the engine speed increases, and continues to run faster, the mixture is too rich. If the engine speed decreases, the mixture is too lean.

㉘ A Unisyn device can be used to measure the air flow accurately so that the carburetors can be balanced more uniformly.

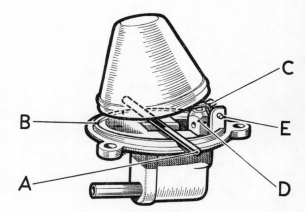

A. ⅛ in. (3·18 mm.) bar.
B. Machined lip.
C. Angle of float lever.
D. Float needle and seat assembly.
E. Lever hinge pin.

Method of checking the float level with the new-style float assembly.

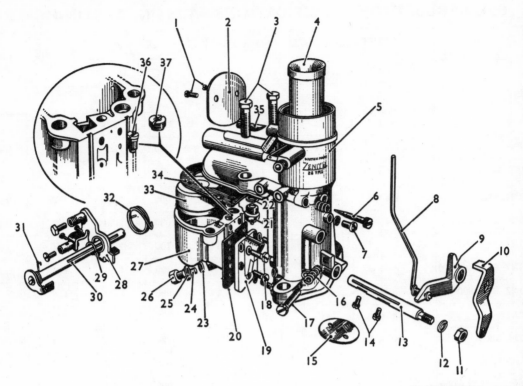

1. Screws fixing strangler flap.
2. Strangler flap.
3. Screws fixing bowl to barrel.
4. Choke tube.
5. Carburetter body.
6. Air regulating screw.
7. Screw fitting choke tube.
8. Interconnection rod.
9. Floating lever.
10. Throttle lever.
11. Throttle lever fixing nut.
12. Spring washer.
13. Throttle spindle.
14. Throttle fixing screws.
15. Throttle.
16. Throttle stop screw spring.
17. Throttle stop screw.
18. Set screws fixing emulsion block.
19. Emulsion block.
20. Gasket for emulsion block.
21. Needle seating.
22. Washer for needle seating.
23. Compensating jet washer.
24. Compensating jet.
25. Main jet washer.
26. Main jet.
27. Float chamber.
28. Strangler lever.
29. Retaining clip for strangler lever.
30. Strangler spindle.
31. Strangler spring.
32. Spring for strangler lever.
33. Float.
34. Gasket (bowl to barrel).
35. Air release tube.
36. Slow running jet.
37. Screw over capacity well.

Exploded view of the Zenith 26 VME carburetor used on the Austin A 40.

ZENITH CARBURETOR SPECIFICATIONS—AUSTIN

MODEL	CARBURETOR MODEL	CHOKE TUBE (Venturi)	MAIN METERING JET	POWER BYPASS JET	FUEL Level (Inch)	FUEL Pressure (Psi)	FLOAT NEEDLE SEAT SIZE mm.	SLOW RUNNING TUBE (Idle)	COM-PENSATING JET	VENT SCREW OVER CAP. WELL	PUMP DISCH. NOZZLE	FAST IDLE Turns ①	FAST IDLE Open ②
	26VME	22	80				1.5	50	57	2.0			
	30VM-6	23	95	100	21/32	1.5	1.5	50	65	2.5		5	#55
A40	30VIG-8	25	90		21/32	1.5	1.5	50	65		50	3	#67
	30VIG-10	25	67		21/32	1.5		50	95		50	3	#67
A50	30VIG-10	27	72		21/32	1.5	1.5	50	95		50	3	#67
A55	30VIG-10	27	72					50	95				

① Number of turns throttle stop screw is turned in from fully closed throttle position.
② Throttle opening with fully closed choke. # indicates drill size.

4

The Electrical System

All of the electrical equipment used on B.M.C. cars is manufactured by Lucas, the service procedures of which are covered in this chapter.

IGNITION SYSTEM

GENERAL INFORMATION

The distributor points are connected to the primary circuit with the spring carrying the primary current to the points. Condensers are conventionally mounted with a single screw. Vacuum advance and mechanical advance units are not adjustable, and the parts must be replaced when the unit does not measure up to specifications.

The distributor caps are somewhat different from ours in that those with horizontal outlets have the high tension wires secured by screws which pierce the insulation and hold the wire securely. In caps with vertical outlets, the cable strands are bent around a washer, and the assembly screwed into the cap. In most caps, the center carbon brush is made of a resistance material for spark suppression.

IDENTIFICATION

Lucas distributors have both a model number and a service number stamped on them. The model number designates the type of distributor while the service number is used for the specifications. The vacuum advance unit has a code number stamped on the body or on the nut for the specifications. This code number consists of three sets of digits separated by hyphens.

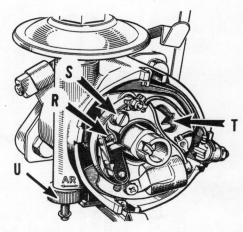

Adjustment screws for the distributor. (R) points, (S) lockscrew, (T) screwdriver pry slot for adjusting the point gap, and (U) the micrometer timing adjustment for various octane rating gasolines.

SERVICING THE DISTRIBUTOR

POINT INSTALLATION

Make sure that the insulation washer is in position between the stationary point bracket and the breaker lever; otherwise, misalignment and grounding will occur. Bend the stationary point bracket for alignment. Spring tension is 18–24 ozs., and

IDENTIFICATION OF LUCAS DISTRIBUTOR CAMS

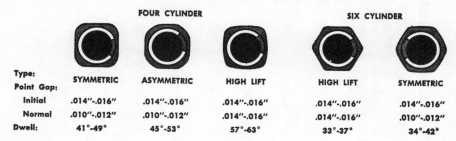

	FOUR CYLINDER			SIX CYLINDER	
Type:	SYMMETRIC	ASYMMETRIC	HIGH LIFT	HIGH LIFT	SYMMETRIC
Point Gap:					
Initial	.014"–.016"	.014"–.016"	.014"–.016"	.014"–.016"	.014"–.016"
Normal	.010"–.012"	.010"–.012"	.014"–.016"	.014"–.016"	.010"–.012"
Dwell:	41°–49°	45°–53°	57°–63°	33°–37°	34°–42°

This shows the various cams that are used in the distributors and specifications for each.

DISTRIBUTOR SPECIFICATIONS—AUSTIN, AUSTIN-HEALEY

MODEL		MANUF. PART NUMBER (Lucas)	ROTA-TION (From Top)	BREAKER POINT GAP		CAM ANGLE (Deg.)	BREAKER ARM SPRING TENSION		CONDENSER CAPACITY (Mfds.)	CENTRIFUGAL ADVANCE (Dist. degrees @ RPM)			VACUUM ADVANCE (Dist. degrees @ RPM)			
				In.	Mm.		Oz.	Gr.		Start	Inter-mediate	Maximum	Code No.	Start (In.)	Max. (In.)	Max. (Deg.)
AUSTIN																
A40-A2S6	LC	40569D/F	CC	.014-.016	.356-.406	45	18-24	500-680	.18-.25	750	9 @ 1300	18 @ 2800	7-14-10	6	20	10.5
	HC	40561E/H	CC	.014-.016	.356-.406	45	18-24	500-680	.18-.25	500	7 @ 900	17 @ 2800	5-12-6	3	18	6.0
A55	LC	40499A	CC	.014-.016	.356-.406	49	18-24	500-680	.18-.25	600	8 @ 1250	18 @ 2800	6-14-8	5	20	8.0
	HC	40570A	CC	.014-.016	.356-.406	49	18-24	500-680	.18-.25	450	7 @ 1130	13 @ 2400	3-13-12	2.5	18	12.0
A55 Mk II	LC	40624D/H	CC	.014-.016	.356-.406	60	18-24	500-680	.18-.25	600	8 @ 1250	17 @ 2800	6-14-8	5	20	8.0
	HC	40643D/H	CC	.014-.016	.356-.406	60	18-24	500-680	.18-.25	450	10 @ 1500	12 @ 2400	5-17-10	4.5	15.5	10.0
850		40648D/H	CC	.014-.016	.356-.016	60	18-24	500-680	.18-.25	350	9 @ 650	17 @ 2200	7-13-5	6	13	5.0

DISTRIBUTOR SPECIFICATIONS—AUSTIN, AUSTIN-HEALEY

MODEL	MANUF. PART NUMBER (Lucas)	ROTATION (From Top)	BREAKER POINT GAP In.	Mm.	CAM ANGLE (Deg.)	BREAKER ARM SPRING TENSION Oz.	Gr.	CONDENSER CAPACITY (Mfds.)	CENTRIFUGAL ADVANCE (Dist. degrees @ RPM) Start	Intermediate	Maximum	VACUUM ADVANCE (Dist. degrees @ RPM) Code No.	Start (In.)	Max. (In.)	Max. (Deg.)
AUSTIN-HEALEY:															
	40320B	CC	.014-.016	.356-.406	38	18-24	500-680	.18-.25	600	9 @ 1250	17 @ 2500	7-18-12	6	25	12.0
BN1	40495A	CC	.014-.016	.356-.406	38	18-24	500-680	.18-.25	600	9 @ 1250	17 @ 2500		7	11.5	6.0
	40422B	CC	.014-.016	.356-.406	38	18-24	500-680	.18-.25	350	9½ @ 750	16 @ 3000	5-17-10	4.5	15.5	10.0
	40520A	CC	.014-.016	.356-.406	38	18-24	500-680	.18-.25	350	9½ @ 750	16 @ 3000	5-17-10	4.5	15.5	10.0
BN4	40532A	CC	.014-.016	.356-.406	38	18-24	500-680	.18-.25	300	8 @ 500	12 @ 1500	5-12-8	4	15	8.0
BN6	40581A	CC	.014-.016	.356-.406	35	18-24	500-680	.18-.25	400	4½ @ 500	15 @ 2000	5-12-8	4	15	8.0
BN7, BT7	40662A	CC	.014-.016	.356-.406	35	18-24	500-680	.18-.25	300	13 @ 1150	15 @ 2000	5-12-8	4	15	8.0
BJ7	40920A/B	CC	.014-.016	.356-.406	35	18-24	500-680	.18-.25	400	7½ @ 650	15 @ 2000	5-12-8	4	15	8.0
BJ8	40966A/B	CC	.014-.016	.356-.406	35	18-24	500-680	.18-.25	500	7½ @ 850	19 @ 3200	5-12-8	4	15	8.0
Sprite	40561E/H	CC	.014-.016	.356-.406	60	18-24	500-680	.18-.25	200	7 @ 900	16 @ 2800	5-12-6	3	18	6.0
Sprite Mk II	40752A	CC	.014-.016	.356-.406	60	18-24	500-680	.18-.25	350	4 @ 700	16 @ 2200	5-12-6	3	18	6.0

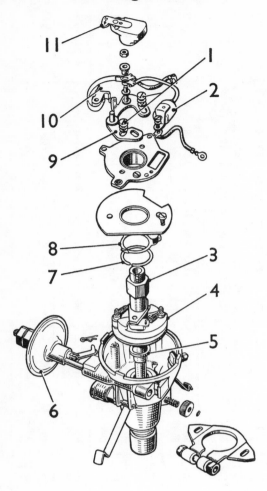

1. *Screws for contact plate.*
2. *Condenser.*
3. *Cam.*
4. *Automatic timing contact.*
5. *Distance collar.*
6. *Vacuum control.*
7. *Felt ring.*
8. *Spring.*
9. *Fixed contact plate.*
10. *Moving contact.*

11. *Rotor.*

An exploded view of an early type distributor.

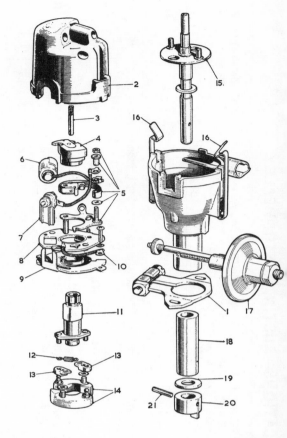

1. Clamping plate.	12. Automatic advance
2. Moulded cap.	springs.
3. Brush and spring.	13. Toggles.
4. Rotor arm.	14. Weight assembly.
5. Contacts (set).	15. Shaft and action plate.
6. Capacitor.	16. Cap-retaining clips.
7. Terminal and lead (low-tension).	17. Vacuum unit.
8. Moving contact breaker plate.	18. Bush.
9. Contact breaker base plate.	19. Thrust washer.
10. Earth lead.	20. Driving dog.
11. Cam.	21. Taper pin.

Exploded view of a late type distributor.

condensers should measure 0.18–0.25 mfds capacity with a leakage rate of not less than 3 megohms. Three types of breaker cams have been used in Lucas distributors: symmetric, asymmetric, and high-lift cams. The cam shapes and the specifications are shown below.

Testing the Advance Curve

Lucas recommends that the distributor be run up to the maximum specified speed, and the advance checked against specifications as the speed is reduced. This is exactly opposite to the method used on American equipment. The vacuum unit is similarly checked against a decreasing vacuum.

SERVICING THE STARTING MOTOR

Disassembling

Remove the cover band, hold back the brush springs, and lift the brushes from their holders. I the starting motor has a field coil terminal protruding from the commutator end bracket, unscrew the terminal nuts from the post. Unscrew the two through-bolts and remove the commutator end bracket from the yoke. Remove the drive-end bracket complete with the armature and starting motor drive assembly. Remove the starter drive mechanism from the armature shaft.

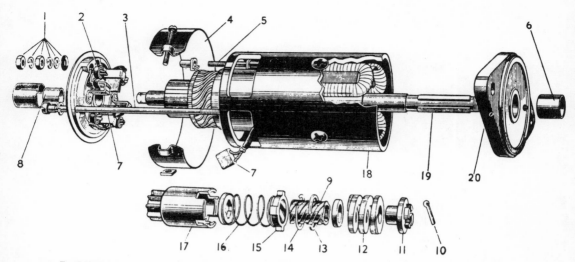

Exploded view of the starting motor. (1) terminal nuts and washers, (2) brush spring, (3) through bolt, (4) cover band, (5) terminal post, (6) bushing, (7) brushes, (8) bushing, (9) sleeve, (10) cotter pin, (11) nut, (12) main spring, (13) retaining ring, (14) washer, (15) control nut, (16) spring, (17) pinion and barrel, (18) yoke, (19) armature shaft, (20) drive end bracket.

Cleaning and Inspecting

Wash all parts in solvent and blow dry. Be careful not to damage the field insulation with compressed air. Make the inspections and electrical tests as described below:

Brush Gear. Brushes must be replaced when worn to ⁵⁄₁₆″ in length. The flexible leads can be unsoldered to replace the brushes. Check the brush spring tension which should be 30–40 ozs. for all models except for the M35G (four-brush model), which should be 32–40 ozs. Two brush holders must be insulated from the frame and two grounded.

Armature. Test the armature windings for open, ground, and shorted coils. A visual inspection can best determine the condition of the windings, especially at the drive end of the armature. Turn the commutator in a lathe but do not undercut the insulation between the segments.

Field Coils. Check the field coils for continuity, shorted windings, and ground. The shorted windings can be detected only by visual inspection of the insulation, as the few turns cannot be measured accurately with an ohmmeter.

Bearings. Always replace the drive-end bushing as it seldom receives lubrication and is subjected to severe stress. Bright sections of the field

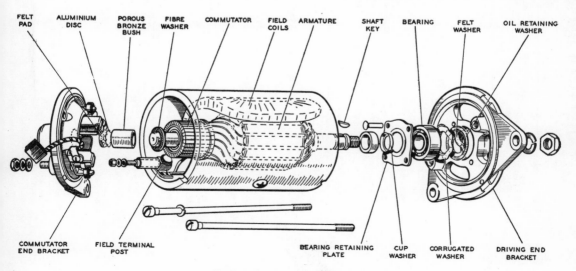

Exploded view of the generator.

GENERATOR AND REGULATOR SPECIFICATIONS—AUSTIN, AUSTIN-HEALEY

MODEL	GENERATOR PART NUMBER (Lucas)	BRUSH SPRING TENSION Ounces	Grams	FIELD Resistance (Ohms)	REGULATOR CUTOUT RELAY PART NUMBER (Lucas)	Follow through In.	Mm.	Point Gap In.	Mm.	Cut-in Voltage	Cut-out Voltage	VOLTAGE REGULATOR (Voltage @ 86°F.)	VOLTAGE AND CURRENT REGULATOR AIR GAP In.	Mm.	CURRENT REGULATOR (Max. Rated Amperes Hot)
AUSTIN:															
A40, A55, 850	C39PV2	22-25	624-709	6.1	RB106/2	.030	.762	.010-.020	.254-.508	12.7-13.3	8.5-11.0	15.9-16.5	.015	.381	
A55 Mk II, A60	C40	30	850	6.0											
AUSTIN-HEALEY:															
BN1, BN2, BN4, BN6, BN7, BT7 & BJ7	C45PV5	24-36	680-1020	6.0	RB106/2	.030	.762	.010-.020	.254-.508	12.7-13.3	8.5-11.0	15.9-16.5	.015	.381	35
BJ8	C42	16-33	450-940	4.5	RB340	.010-.020	.25-.51	.035-.045	.90-1.04	12.6-13.4	9.3-11.2	14.5-15.1	.045-.049	1.04-1.24	
Sprite Mk I & II	C40	30	850	6.0	RB106/2	.030	.762	.010-.020	.254-.508	12.7-13.3	8.5-11.0	15.9-16.5	.015	.381	

STARTER AND BATTERY SPECIFICATIONS—AUSTIN, AUSTIN-HEALEY

MODEL	STARTER PART NUMBER (Lucas)	BRUSH SPRING TENSION Ounces	Grams	FREE RUNNING TEST Max. Amps.	Min. Volts	Min. Rpm	RESISTANCE TEST Max. Amps.	Min. Volts	Torque Ft.Lbs.	M. Kg.	Rpm	LOCK TEST Max. Amps.	Min. Volts	Torque Ft.Lbs.	M.Kg.	VOLTS	BATTERY TERMINAL GROUNDED P-Positive N-Negative	CAPACITY (Ampere hour @ 20 hour rate)	GROUP NUMBER Lucas	S.A.E.	AABM
AUSTIN:																					
A40, A55, 850	M35G	32-40	906-1133	45	12	9500	270	8.8	5.4	.75	1000	440	7.4	10	1.38	12	P	43	BTZ7A	2SM	24S
A60	M35G	32-40	906-1133	45	12	9500	270	8.8	5.4	.75	1000	440	7.4	10	1.38	12	P	58	BTZ9A	2SM	27S
AUSTIN-HEALEY:																					
BN1, BN2, & BN4	M418G	32-40	906-1133	45	12	5800	270	9.0	8.0	1.1	1000	460	7.0	17	2.35	6(2)	P	58	SLG11E (2)	2SM	27S
BN6, BN7, BT7, BJ7 & BJ8	M418G	32-40	906-1133	45	12	5800	270	9.0	8.0	1.1	1000	460	7.0	17	2.35	6(2)	P	58	BTZ9A	2SM	27S
Sprite Mk I, II, & III	M35G	32-40	906-1133	45	12	9500	270	8.8	5.4	.75	1000	440	7.4	10	1.38	12	P	43	BTZ7A ①	2SM	24S

① An N9 battery was used in the Sprite Mk II, and Mk III.

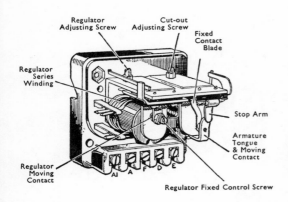

Regulator Adjusting Screw — Cut-out Adjusting Screw — Fixed Contact Blade — Regulator Series Winding — Stop Arm — Armature Tongue & Moving Contact — Regulator Moving Contact — A1 A F D E — Regulator Fixed Control Screw

The RB 106/2 regulator. (1) regulator adjusting screw, (2) cutout adjusting screw.

pole pieces are evidence that the armature has been rubbing because of an excessively worn bushing.

ASSEMBLING

Assembly is the reverse of disassembly.

SERVICING THE GENERATOR

DISASSEMBLING

The generators are similar in construction to American units; therefore, no difficulty should ensue. First remove the driving pulley. Unscrew the two through-bolts. Lift off the commutator end bracket, and then remove the drive-end bracket together with the armature. Be careful not to lose the fiber thrust washer. Press the armature from the drive-end bearing. Remove the brushes and springs from the commutator end bracket.

CLEANING AND INSPECTING

ARMATURE. Clean the armature with a rag dampened with solvent. Do not dip the armature in solvent or you will short the coils. Turn the commutator in a lathe, and then undercut the mica 1/32". Test the armature for ground, shorted coils, or an open circuit.

FIELD COILS. Wipe the field housing with a rag dampened with solvent. Do not soak the fields in solvent or the insulation will be softened. Check the field coils for continuity, and ground. Measure the resistance of the field coils and compare it with specifications.

BRUSH HOLDERS. Clean the brush holder assembly with solvent. Test the brush holders for ground; one holder should be grounded and the other insulated. In general, brushes should be replaced when the generator is overhauled.

ASSEMBLING

Assembly is the reverse of disassembly.

REGULATORS—TYPES RF95, RF96, RB106-1 AND RB106-2

These regulators are dual units containing a cutout and voltage regulator. No current regulator relay is used. When the voltage rises to the setting of the regulator, a resistance is inserted into the field circuit for control. To prevent damage to the generator when the battery charge is low, and the current drain large, a series winding is provided around the voltage coil to add magnetic force and cause the voltage relay to operate, thus doing the work of the missing current regulator. The service problems and adjustments are similar to American regulators with the exception that the voltage tests and adjustments are made on an open circuit. One adjustment compensates for both voltage and current.

VOLTAGE REGULATOR TEST

Remove the wires from the terminals marked "A" and "A1" at the control box and join them together. Connect the negative lead of a voltmeter to the control box terminal "D" and the other lead to terminal "E." Start the engine and increase its speed until the meter needle flickers and then remains steady. This should occur between the limits given in the Generator Specification table.

VOLTAGE REGULATOR ADJUSTMENT

Stop the engine, remove the control box cover, and loosen the locknut holding the adjusting screw. Turn the adjusting screw in a clockwise direction a fraction of a turn at a time to raise the setting. Tighten the locknut each time before rechecking. *CAUTION: The testing should be completed within 30 seconds, otherwise the shunt winding will overheat and give a false reading.*

CUTOUT TEST

Connect a voltmeter between the control box terminals D and E. Remove the cover in order to note the instant of point closure. Switch on the headlamps so that the drain will cause a slight drop in the voltmeter reading. Start the engine and slowly increase its speed. Note the voltage when the generator "cuts in." Reduce engine speed and note the point where the needle returns to zero. The lowest reading, just before the needle jumps back, is the "drop-off" voltage. If an ammeter is hooked into the armature-to-regulator "D" circuit, after disconnecting the wire, the reverse current can be determined at the same time the "drop-off" voltage is read. The readings should be within the range given in the Generator Specification table.

CUTOUT ADJUSTMENT

To adjust the cut-in voltage, loosen the locknut and turn the adjustment screw in a clockwise direction to raise the voltage setting. Turn the screw only a fraction of a turn at a time and then

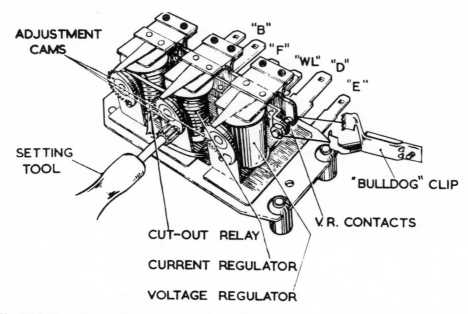

ADJUSTMENT CAMS

"B"
"F"
"WL" "D"
"E"

SETTING TOOL

"BULLDOG" CLIP

V.R. CONTACTS

CUT-OUT RELAY

CURRENT REGULATOR

VOLTAGE REGULATOR

The RB 340 regulator. Note the use of the bulldog clip to short out the voltage regulator for adjusting the current regulator. Turn the adjusting tool clockwise to raise the settings.

tighten the locknut. Test after each adjustment by increasing the engine speed and noting the voltmeter reading at the instant of contact closure. Electrical settings of the cut-out, like the regulator, must be made as quickly as possible because of temperature-rise effects. Tighten the locknut after making the adjustment.

To adjust the "drop-off" voltage, stop the engine and remove the control box cover. Adjust the height of the fixed contact by carefully bending the fixed contact blade toward the armature to reduce the drop-off voltage or away from it to raise the drop-off voltage. Recheck the setting and, if necessary, re-adjust until the correct drop-off setting is obtained. Restore the original connections and install the cover.

REGULATORS, TYPES RB 310 AND 340

These regulators consist of three units: a cutout, a voltage regulator, and a current regulator. They are very similar in construction to current American practice. However, they can be used with either positive or negative grounded circuits by polarizing them at the time of installation, except those units with a diode.

VOLTAGE REGULATOR TEST

Disconnect the wire leading to the control box terminal B. Connect a voltmeter to the D terminal and the ground. Increase the engine speed until the generator speed is 3,000 rpm and note the open-circuit voltage, which should be as follows for the RB 310:

TEMPERATURE	6-VOLT UNITS	12-VOLT UNITS	24-VOLT UNITS
50°F. (10°C.)	8.1–8.5	15.1–15.7	28.7–29.2
68°F. (20°C.)	8.0–8.4	14.9–15.5	28.4–28.9
86°F. (30°C.)	7.9–8.3	14.7–15.3	28.1–28.6
104°F. (40°C.)	7.8–8.2	14.5–15.1	27.8–28.3

For the RB 340, the voltage should be within the following limits:

TEMPERATURE	SETTING
50°F. (10°C.)	14.9–15.5
68°F. (20°C.)	14.7–15.3
86°F. (30°C.)	14.5–15.1
104°F. (40°C.)	14.3–14.9

VOLTAGE REGULATOR ADJUSTMENT

If the reading is outside of specifications, loosen the locknut of the voltage regulator and turn the adjustment screw clockwise with the special setting tool to raise the voltage. Recheck and then re-connect the wire to terminal B. *CAUTION: Testing must be completed within 30 seconds to avoid heating the shunt coil which would change the values.*

CURRENT REGULATOR TEST

To make the generator charge at its maximum rating, short circuit the voltage regulator contacts with a bulldog clip as shown, and then disconnect the wire from terminal B and connect a 0–40 ammeter between the wire and terminal B on the regulator box. Run the engine at about 2,700 rpm and the generator should register its maximum output as indicated in the generator specification table.

Current Regulator Adjustment

Loosen the locknut of the current regulator and turn it clockwise to raise the setting as required. The same 30-second limit must be adhered to in this adjustment also.

Cutout Tests

Connect a voltmeter between the regulator box terminals D and B. Start the engine and increase its speed *slowly* while watching the voltmeter needle, which will rise gradually and suddenly dip as the contact points come together. This is the "cut-in" voltage. Reduce speed slowly and note the last point just before the needle rises sharply, which is the "drop-off" voltage. The readings should be within the following limits:

	Cut-in Voltage	Drop-off Voltage
6-volt units:	6.3– 6.7	4.8– 5.5
12-volt units:	12.7–13.3	9.5–11.0
24-volt units:	26.5–27.0	19.0–23.0

Cutout Adjustment

To raise the cut-in voltage, loosen the locknut and turn the adjustment screw clockwise a fraction of a turn at a time. Tighten the locknut after each adjustment. This test must also be carried out quickly.

AUXILIARY ELECTRICAL EQUIPMENT

Electric windshield wipers and a brake override relay are also part of many Lucas circuits. The windshield wipers contain the usual electric motor and gearing arrangement. However, the current specifications are different. The brake override relay is unique and used only where one bulb has to do the work of both the stop and turn signal lights. The relay operates to permit one rear light to flash and the other to remain lit.

ELECTRIC WINDSHIELD WIPER

Disassembling

Withdraw the four screws holding the gearbox cover and remove the cover. Withdraw the terminal screws and the through-bolts at the commutator end bracket and remove the bracket. The brush gear can now be removed by lifting it clear of the commutator and withdrawing it as a unit. Care must be taken to note the particular side occupied by each for assembly purposes. Access to the armature and field coils can be gained by withdrawing the yoke. If it is necessary to remove the field coil, unscrew the two screws holding the pole piece at the yoke. These screws should be marked so that they can be replaced in their original holes. Press out the pole pieces complete with field coil, marking each pole piece so that it can be properly replaced. Press the pole pieces from the field coil.

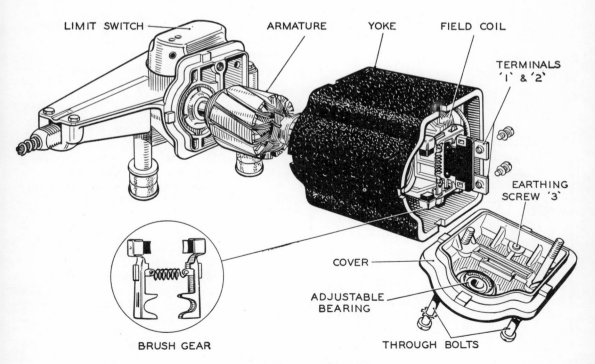

Parts of the electric windshield wiper.

TROUBLESHOOTING

If the wiper operates unsatisfactorily, check the current being drawn by the motor.

If the wiper takes no current, examine the fuse as it may be blown. Check the wiring before replacing the fuse or the new one will blow out, too. If the wiper contains a thermostat (circuit breaker), remove the wires and check across the terminals with an ohmmeter. A closed circuit means that the thermostat is good. An open circuit means that the unit has not reset itself. Check by substituting a new thermostat. Do not attempt to repair the unit.

If the wiper takes abnormally low current, check the battery for a full charge. Remove the commutator end bracket and examine the brush gear. The commutator must be clean and the brushes bear properly on the commutator. Check out a suspected armature by substitution.

If the wiper takes abnormally high current, the load is excessive. It may be caused by misalignment of the gear shafts or lack of armature end play, which should be 0.008" (0.20 mm.) to 0.012" (0.30 mm.). Carbon brush particles may be shorting the commutator segments. The resistance between adjacent commutator segments and the field resistance should be checked against the specification sheet. Frictional losses may also be caused by badly positioned or defective connecting tubes. Check the tubing for sharp bends or obstructions. A normal tube will have no more than 6 lbs. tension.

BRAKE SWITCH OVERRIDE RELAY

An override relay is incorporated in some circuits to prevent simultaneous application of the brake and direction signal lights. When simultaneous application is made, the override relay operates to allow the proper stop light filament to flash and the other to remain steady.

TROUBLESHOOTING

In the event troubleshooting is necessary, check

The fuse and flasher units are located on the firewall. The smaller cars use two 35 amp. fuses, while some of the larger cars are equipped with one 35 amp. and one 50 amp. fuse.

the bulb filaments. Turn on the ignition and measure the voltage at the flasher unit terminal B which should be the same as the battery voltage; otherwise, use the wiring diagram to check the wiring leading to the relay. Connect the flasher unit terminals B and L together and operate the turn indicator switch. If the flasher lamps now light, the flasher unit is defective. If the lamps do not light, test the brake switch override relay as follows:

TROUBLESHOOTING THE BRAKE OVERRIDE RELAY

Use a jumper wire to connect terminals 1, 2, and 3 together; the left-hand lamps should now flash. Use the jumper wire to connect relay terminals 1, 6, and 7 together; the right-hand lamps should now flash.

INSTALLING A NEW FLASHER UNIT

When replacing a flasher unit, it is advisable to test the circuit to avoid damaging the new flasher unit. Join the cables normally connected to flasher terminals L, B, and P together and operate the direction-indicator switch. In the event there is trouble in the line or an incorrect connection made, the ignition auxiliary fuse will blow out but no damage will result to the flasher unit.

ADJUSTING THE RELAY AIR GAPS

Each armature controls three pairs of contacts, two pairs being normally open and one pair normally closed. For setting purposes, the three contacts can be identified as follows: Inner pairs, next to the core, normally open; outer lower pairs, normally open; outer upper pairs, normally closed. When an inner pair of contacts is just touching, a

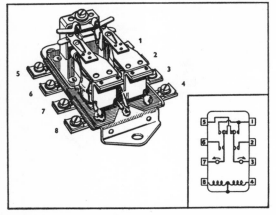

The brake override relay and its wiring diagram in the inset.

LIGHT BULBS—AUSTIN, AUSTIN-HEALEY

CAR MODEL	MANUF.	HEAD LAMPS		PARKING	TAIL	STOP	DIRECTION SIGNALS			LICENSE PLATE	INSTRU-MENT	IGNITION
		Outer	Indicator				Front	Rear	Indicator			
AUSTIN:												
A40, A55, A60, 850	Lucas		987	989	380	380	382	382	987	222 989	987	987
	U. S.	6012	1446	57	1034	1034	1141	1141	1446	57 1891	1446	1446
AUSTIN-HEALEY:												
BN1, BN2	Lucas	354	987	361	361	361	361	361	987	222	987	
	U. S.	6012	1446	1034	1034	1034	1034	1034	1446	57	1446	
BN4, BN6, BN7, BT7, BJ7, & BJ8	Lucas		987	380	380	380	382	382	987	222		987
	U. S.	6012	1446	1034	1034	1034	1034	1034	1446	57 1891		1446
Sprite Mk I, II, & III	Lucas		987	380	380	380	382	382	987	989	987	
	U. S.	6012	1446	1034	1034	1034	1034	1141	1446	57 1891	1446	

relay should have an armature-to-core-gap of 0.010″–0.015″. And when these contacts are separated by 0.007″–0.013″ gap, the outer lower contacts must be separated by 0.012″–0.018″ gap. Adjustments are made by bending the fixed contact carrier as follows: (1) Insert a 0.010″ gauge between an armature and its core. (2) Press down on the armature. (3) Adjust the height of the inner contact carrier until the inner pair of contacts is just touching. (4) Remove the gauge. (5) Insert the 0.010″ gauge between the inner pair of contacts and lightly press down on the armature. (6) Adjust the outer lower contact carrier until the outer lower contacts are just touching. (7) Remove the gauge. (8) With the outer lower contacts just touching, adjust the upper contact carrier until a 0.015″ gauge is a sliding fit between the outer upper contacts. (9) Remove the gauge and install the cover.

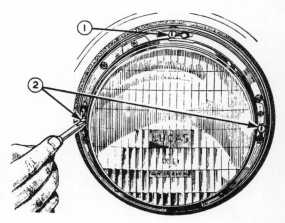

Headlamp aiming screws. (1) vertical adjustment, (2) horizontal adjustment.

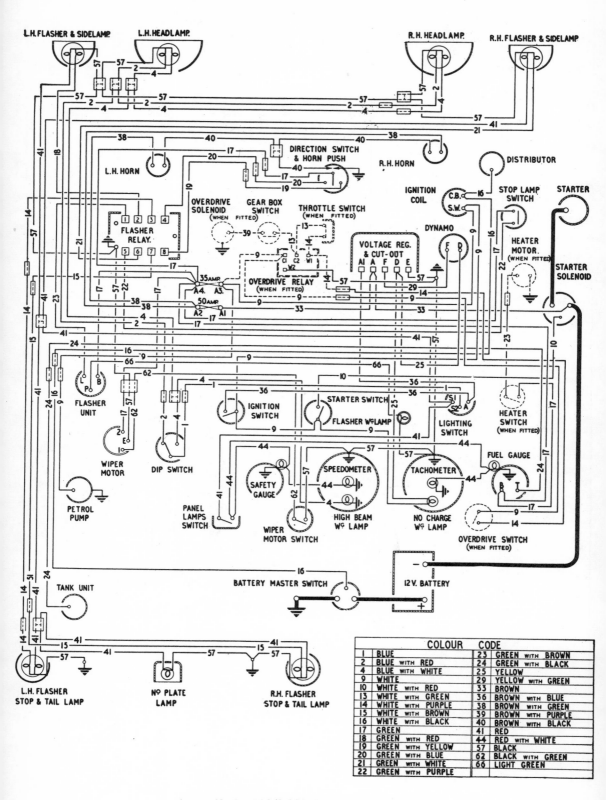

Austin-Healey 100/3,000 chassis wiring diagram.

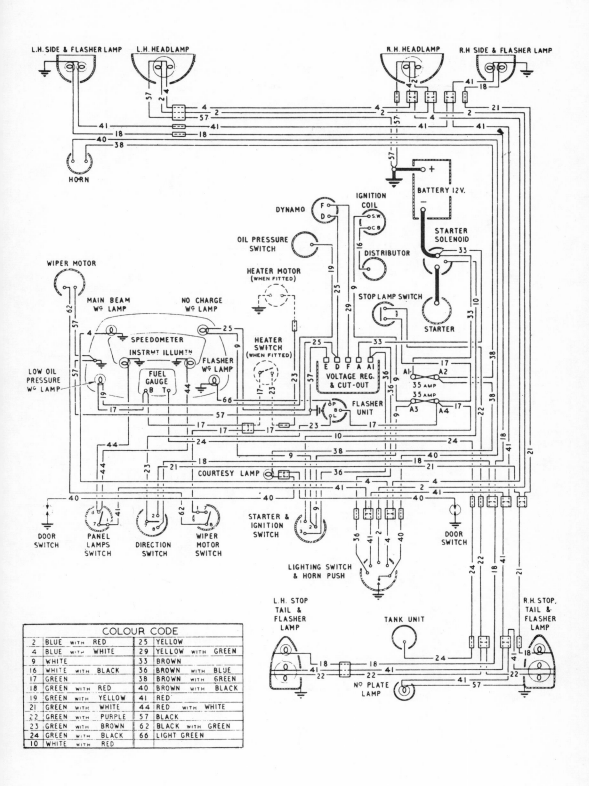

Chassis wiring diagram of the Austin A 40.

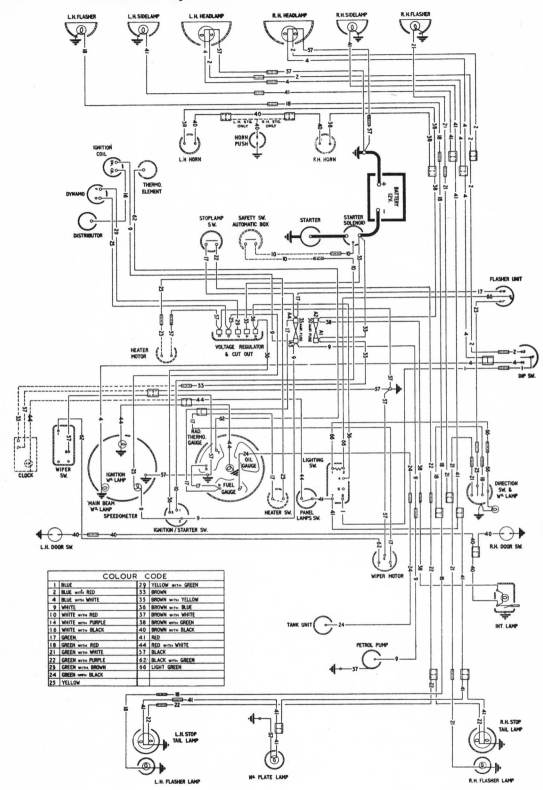

Chassis wiring diagram of the Austin A 55.

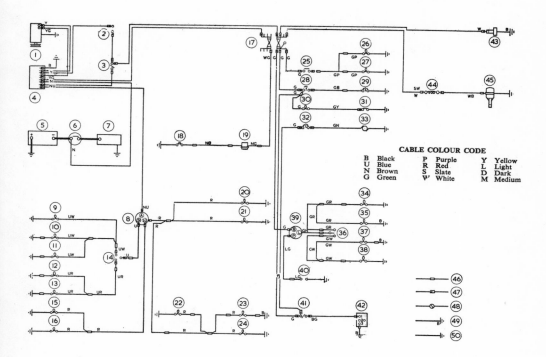

CABLE COLOUR CODE

B	Black	P	Purple	Y	Yellow	
U	Blue	R	Red	L	Light	
N	Brown	S	Slate	D	Dark	
G	Green	W	White	M	Medium	

1.	Dynamo.	18.	Horn-push.	35.	L/H front flasher.
2.	Ignition warning light.	19.	Horn.	36.	Flasher switch.
3.	Ignition switch.	20.	Panel light.	37.	R/H front flasher.
4.	Control box.	21.	Panel light.	38.	R/H rear flasher.
5.	12-volt battery.	22.	R/H tail lamp.	39.	Flasher unit.
6.	Starter switch.	23.	Number-plate lamp.	40.	Flasher warning light.
7.	Starter motor.	24.	L/H tail lamp.	41.	Screen wiper switch.
8.	Lighting switch.	25.	Stop lamp switch.	42.	Screen wiper motor.
9.	Main beam warning light.	26.	R/H stop lamp.	43.	Fuel pump.
10.	R/H headlamp main beam.	27.	L/H stop lamp.	44.	Ignition coil.
11.	L/H headlamp main beam.	28.	Fuel gauge.	45.	Distributor.
12.	R/H headlamp dip beam.	29.	Fuel tank unit.	46.	Snap connectors.
13.	L/H headlamp dip beam.	30.	Oil pressure indicator lamp.	47.	Lucar connectors.
14.	Dipper switch.	31.	Oil pressure switch.	48.	Terminal blocks or junction box.
15.	L/H sidelamp.	32.	Heater rheostat.	49.	Earth connections made via cable.
16.	R/H sidelamp.	33.	Heater motor.	50.	Earth connections via fixing bolts.
17.	Fuse unit.	34.	L/H rear flasher.		

Chassis wiring diagram of the Austin 850.

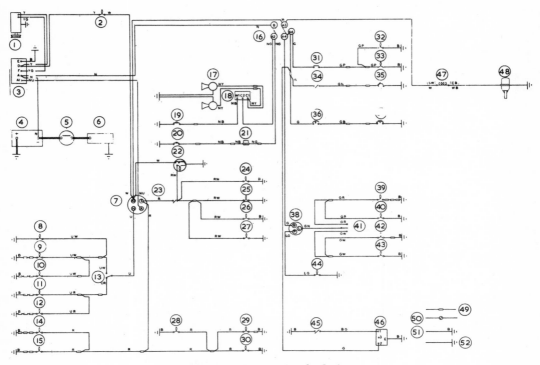

Chassis wiring diagram for the Sprite.

1. Generator.	18. Horn Relay.	36. Fuel Gauge.
2. Ignition Warning Light.	19. Horn Push.	37. Fuel Gauge Tank Unit.
3. Control Box.	20. Horn Push.	38. Flasher Unit.
4. 12-volt Battery.	21. Horn.	39. L/H Front Flasher.
5. Starter Switch.	22. Cigar Lighter & Illumination.	40. L H Rear Flasher.
6. Starter Motor.	23. Panel Light Switch	41. Flasher Switch.
7. Lighting and Ignition Switch.	24. Panel Light.	42. R/H Rear Flasher.
8. Main Beam Warning Light.	25. Speedometer Light.	43. R H Front Flasher.
9. R/H Headlamp Main Beam.	26. Panel Light.	44. Flasher Warning Light.
10. L/H Headlamp Main Beam.	27. Tachometer Light (when fitted)	45. Windshield Switch.
11. L/H Headlamp Dip Beam.	28. R/H Tail Lamp.	46. Windshield Wipers.
12. R/H Headlamp Dip Beam.	29. Number Plate Lamp.	47. Ignition Coil.
13. Dipper Switch.	30. L/H Tail Lamp.	48. Distributor.
14. L/H Sidelamp.	31. Stop Lamp Switch.	49. Snap Connectors.
15. R/H Sidelamp.	32. R/H Stop Lamp.	50. Terminal Blocks or Junction Box.
16. Fuse Unit.	33. L/H Stop Lamp.	51. Earth Connections made via Cable or
17. Connections for Twin Windtone Horns (when fitted)	34. Heater Switch ⎫ when fitted	52. Via Fixing Bolts.
	35. Heater Motor ⎭	

Key to the Sprite chassis wiring diagram.

5

Engine Service

DESCRIPTION OF A TYPICAL BMC ENGINE

BMC engine design revolves about a four-cylinder, in-line engine, with overhead valves. A similarly constructed engine, with six cylinders, is used in the Austin-Healey. These engines are made in a variety of capacities to suit the power requirements of the car. Engine service techniques are alike, regardless of engine size and car model.

The valves are set in line in the cylinder head and are operated by rocker arms and push rods from a camshaft in the left-hand side of the block. Oil seals are installed on the valves, and there is the normal provision for adjustment. The camshaft is chain driven and is provided with a synthetic rubber, slipper-type tensioner. The oil pump and distributor are driven by the camshaft.

The pistons are aluminum alloy with three compression rings and a slotted oil control ring. The piston pins are clamped in the connecting rods, although some later models are full floating.

Three replaceable main bearings support the crankshaft. The end thrust is taken by special washers at the center main bearing. A replaceable oil filter element is housed on the right-hand side of the engine.

A centrifugal-type water pump and fan are driven from the crankshaft pulley by the generator belt.

ROCKER ARM SHAFT ASSEMBLY

Four of the nuts holding the rocker arm shaft to the cylinder head also retain the head; therefore, it is essential to drain the coolant before removing the rocker arm shaft assembly. Loosen all the cylinder head nuts evenly to avoid distorting the head. Remove the four remaining rocker arm shaft bracket nuts, and then remove the assembly complete with the brackets. Withdraw the push rods and store them carefully so that they can be replaced in their original positions on assembly.

To disassemble the rocker arm shaft, first remove the set screw which locates the shaft in the rear bracket, and then remove the cotter pins, flat washers, and spring washers from each end of the shaft. Slide the rocker arms, brackets, and springs from the shaft.

When replacing the rocker arm shaft bushings, make sure that the split in the bushing lines up with a point just above the oil hole on the adjusting screw side. When the bushing is in position, remove the small plug from the end of this oil hole and use a 0.093" (2.355 mm.) drill to drill through the bushing. Use a No. 47, 0.0785" (1.98 mm.) drill in the second oil hole on top of the rocker arm and drill through the bushing. After fitting the bushing to the shaft with a running clearance of 0.002" (0.0508 mm.), replug the hole on the adjusting screw side with a new plug, which should be welded into position.

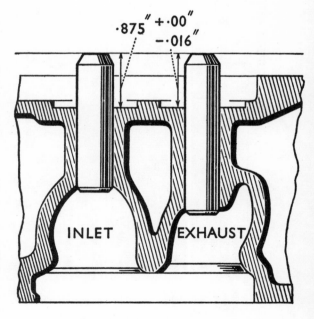

INLET   EXHAUST

Correct positions for new valve guides, Austin-Healey BN1, BN2, BN4, BN6, BN7, & BT7.

VALVE SPECIFICATIONS—AUSTIN, AUSTIN-HEALEY

MODEL	FACE ANGLE (Degs.) Int. & Exh.	RUNNING CLEARANCE H=Hot C=Cold In.	RUNNING CLEARANCE Mm.	VALVE TIMING Intake opens before TDC (Degs.)	Clearance for checking valve timing In.	Clearance for checking Mm.	LIFT In.	LIFT Mm.	Number of teeth between sprocket marks	PRESSURE Inner Lbs.@in. of length	Inner Kg.@mm. of length	Outer Lbs.@in. of length	Outer Kg.@mm. of length	Assembled height In.	Assembled height Mm.	DIAMETER Intake In.	Intake Mm.	Exhaust In.	Exhaust Mm.	CLEARANCE Intake In.	Intake Mm.	Exhaust In.	Exhaust Mm.	VALVE GUIDE Installed height In.	Mm.
AUSTIN:																									
A40, A256	45	.012C	.305C	5	.019	.48	.285	7.24	O.C.											.0015-.0025	.0381-.0635	.002-.003	.051-.076		
A55	45	.012H	.305H	5	.021	.53	.312	7.93	O.C.			37@1.30	17@32.9			.3422-.3427	8.691-8.704	.34175-.34225	8.680-8.693	.0015-.0025	.038-.063	.002-.003	.051-.076	.625	15.87
A55 Mk II	45	.015H	.380H	5	.021	.53	.312	7.93	O.C.							.3422-.3427	8.691-8.704	.34175-.34225	8.680-8.693	.0015-.0025	.038-.063	.002-.003	.051-.076	.625	15.87
A60	45	.015H	.380H	5	.021	.53	.312	7.93	O.C.	30@1.44	13.6@36.51	62@1.56	28.1@39.69	1 9/16	39.69	.3422-.3427	8.691-8.704	.34175-.34225	8.680-8.693	.0015-.0025	.038-.063	.002-.003	.051-.076	.625	15.87
580	45	.012C	.305C	5	.019	.48	.285	7.24	O.C.							.2793-.2798	7.096-7.109	.2788-.2793	7.081-7.096	.0015-.0025	.038-.063	.0010-.0019	.025-.048		
AUSTIN-HEALEY:																									
BN1, BN2	45	.012C	.305C	5	.021	.53	.390	9.91	O.C.	22@1.50	10.2@38.1	65@1.71	29.5@43.3	1.703	43.25	.34175-.34225	8.680-8.693	.34175-.34225	8.680-8.693	.0015-.0025	.038-.068	.001-.002	.025-.051	.875	22.23
BN4	45①	.012C	.305C	5	.023	.61	.315	8.05	O.C.	25@1.52	11.5@38.5	54@1.61	24.6@40.1	1.607	40.82	.34175-.34225	8.680-8.693	.34175-.34225	8.680-8.693	.0015-.0025	.038-.068	.001-.002	.025-.051	.875	22.23
BN6	45	.012C	.305C	5	.023	.61	.315	8.05	O.C.	44@1.60	19.7@40.1	56@1.51	25.2@38.2	1.504	38.20	.34175-.34225	8.680-8.693	.34175-.34225	8.680-8.693	.0015-.0025	.038-.063	.001-.002	.025-.051	.875	22.23
BN7, BT7	45	.012C②	.305C	5	.023	.61	.315	8.05	O.C.	26@1.51	11.8@38.2	56@1.60	25.2@40.5	1.594	40.49	.34175-.34225	8.680-8.693	.34175-.34225	8.680-8.693	.0015-.0025	.038-.063	.001-.002	.025-.051	.875	22.23
BJ7 Mk II	45	.012C	.305C	10	.023	.61	.368	9.36	O.C.	26@1.51	11.8@38.2	67.5@1.60	30.6@40.5	1.594	40.49	.34175-.34225	8.680-8.693	.34175-.34225	8.680-8.693	.0015-.0025	.038-.063	.001-.002	.025-.051	1.348③	34.23③
BJ8 Mk III	45	.012C	.305C	16	.023	.61	.368	9.36	O.C.	26@1.51	11.8@38.2	67.5@1.60	30.6@40.5	1.594	40.49	.34175-.34225	8.680-8.693	.34175-.34225	8.680-8.693	.0015-.0025	.038-.063	.001-.002	.025-.051	1.348③	34.23③
Sprite	45				.019	.48	.280	7.14				52@1.30	23.6@32.8	1.291	32.79	.2793-.2798	7.094-7.107	.2788-.2793	7.081-7.094	.0015-.0025	.038-.063	.002-.003	.051-.076	19/32	15.10
Sprite Mk II & Mk III	45	.012H②	.305H	5	.021	.533	.285	7.24	O.C.																

① Intake valve 30° with 4-port head.
② Set valve clearance to 0.015"H (0.381 mm.) for racing.
③ Value is for intake valve guide. The exhaust valve guide should extend 1.036" (26.32 mm.) above the head.

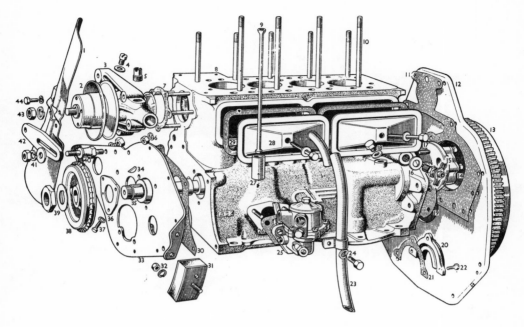

Details of the cylinder block of a BMC engine.

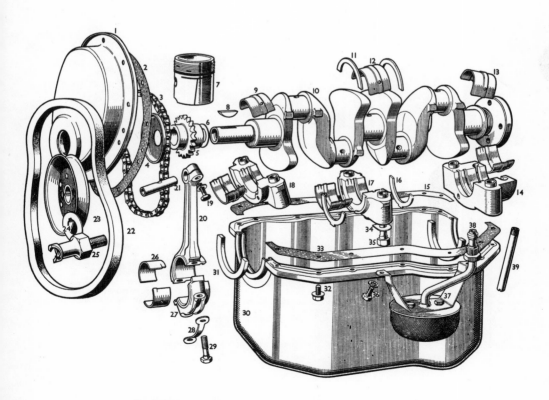

Exploded view of the crankshaft and timing chain assembly.

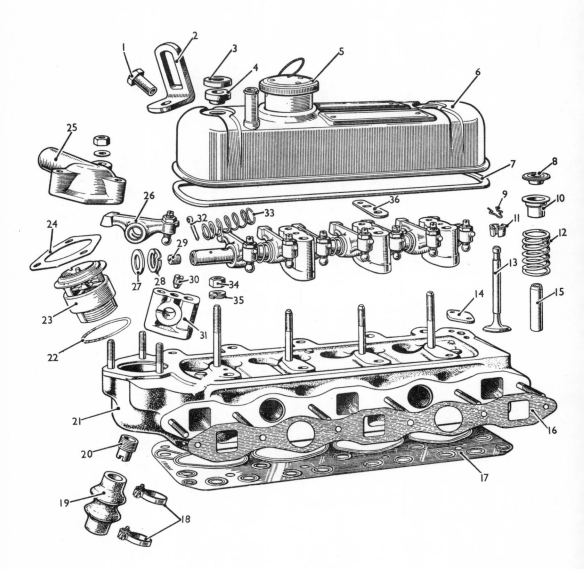

1. Valve rocker cover cap nut.	13. Valve.	25. Water outlet elbow.
2. Engine sling bracket.	14. Cover plate.	26. Rocker.
3. Cup washer.	15. Valve guide.	27. Plain washer.
4. Rubber bush.	16. Joint washer.	28. Spring washer.
5. Oil filler cap.	17. Gasket.	29. Rocker shaft plug.
6. Valve rocker cover.	18. Hose clips.	30. Locating grub screw.
7. Rocker cover joint washer.	19. By-pass hose.	31. Rocker shaft pedestal.
8. Valve spring cap.	20. By-pass tube.	32. Split pin
9. Valve cotter circlip	21. Cylinder head.	33. Rocker spacing spring.
10. Valve oil seal retainer.	22. Thermostat joint washer.	34. Rocker bracket nut.
11. Valve cotters.	23. Thermostat.	35. Rocker bracket washer.
12. Valve spring.	24. Water outlet elbow joint washer.	36. Rocker bracket plate.

Details of the cylinder head and valve mechanism.

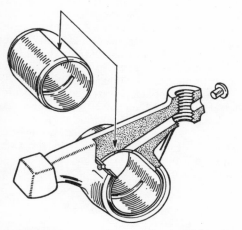

When installing a new rocker arm bushing, make sure that the seam is at the top as shown.

VALVES

The valves are held in position with a pair of half-moon keepers retained by a horseshoe clip. An "O" ring oil seal is used under the retainer to keep oil from passing into the combustion chamber. The "O" rings are easier to install if they have been soaked in engine oil for a short period.

VALVE GUIDES

Valve guides are replaceable and pressed in the cylinder head. The distance that the new guides must extend above the head is given in the Valve Specification table, as it varies with car models. When installing new guides, they must be pressed in from the top of the head. The inlet guide must be inserted with the end having the largest chamfer at the top, and the exhaust guides should have their counterbored ends at the bottom. *NOTE: The ex-*

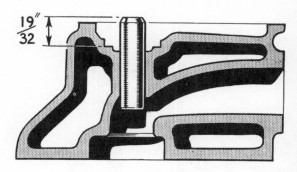

Specifications for pressing new valve guides into the Sprite cylinder head.

haust valve guides are longer than the intake guides.

TIMING CHAIN SERVICE

To remove a chain which is held in position by a hydraulic tensioner, remove the bottom plug from the chain tensioner body and insert a ⅛" (3.18 mm.) Allen wrench, which should be turned clockwise until the rubber slipper is completely free of spring pressure. Between a half and one full turn is all that is required.

The two timing gears can now be removed with the timing chain by alternately easing each gear forward a little at a time. Be careful not to lose the washers behind the crankshaft gear which is the alignment adjustment. If new crankshaft parts are to be installed, the gear alignment adjustment must be made as follows:

Place a straightedge across the sides of the cam-

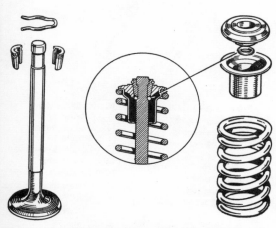

The valve assembly. The inset shows the proper method of installing the oil seal.

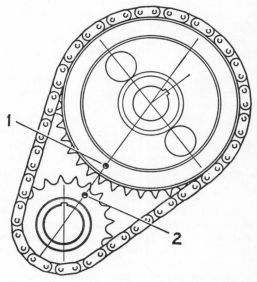

The timing chain marks must align through the shaft centers.

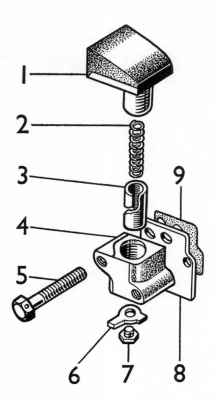

is held against the chain by the coil spring. Should the chain stretch with use, the plunger will rise and the limiting peg, bearing on the top of the helical slot, will rotate the cylinder until the next recess in the lower edge of the slot comes into line with the limiting peg, which prevents the plunger from returning to its original position.

When reassembling, insert the spring into the plunger and place the cylinder on the other end of the spring. Compress the spring until the cylinder enters the plunger bore, engaging the helical slot with the peg in the plunger. Hold the assembly compressed in this position and insert the Allen wrench. Turn the wrench clockwise until the end

1.	Slipper head.	5.	Setpin.
2.	Spring.	6.	Lockwasher.
3.	Locating sleeve.	7.	Plug.
4.	Body.	8.	Backplate.
	9. Joint washer.		

Exploded view of the timing chain tensioner.

shaft gear teeth and measure the gap between the straightedge and the side of the crankshaft gear. Subtract 0.005″ (0.13 mm.) from the feeler gauge reading, which is the correct thickness of washers that should be positioned behind the crankshaft gear.

Mesh the two gears so that the markings line up between shaft centers. After the chain is in place, release the timing chain tensioner by inserting the Allen wrench and turning it clockwise until the slipper head moves forward against the chain under spring pressure. *CAUTION: Do not attempt to turn the wrench counterclockwise or force the slipper head into the chain by external pressure.*

CHAIN TENSIONER ASSEMBLY DETAILS

To disassemble the tensioner, engage the lower end of the cylinder with the Allen wrench and turn it clockwise while holding the wrench and plunger securely until the cylinder and spring are released from inside of the plunger.

When the engine is in operation, oil enters the back face under pressure and lubricates the bearing surface through a hole in the slipper pad. The pad

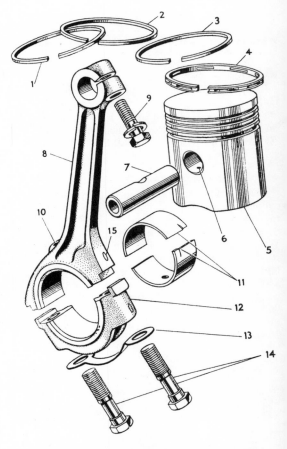

1.	Piston ring—parallel.	10.	Cylinder wall lubricating jet.
2.	Piston ring—taper.	11.	Connecting rod bearing.
3.	Piston ring—taper.		
4.	Piston ring—scraper.	12.	Connecting rod cap.
5.	Piston.	13.	Lock washer.
6.	Gudgeon pin lubricating hole.	14.	Set screws.
7.	Gudgeon pin.	15.	Connecting rod and cap marking.
8.	Connecting rod.		
9.	Clamping screw and washer.		

Details of the piston and rod assembly. The clamp bolt was replaced by two lock rings in 1962.

ENGINE TORQUE SPECIFICATIONS—AUSTIN, AUSTIN-HEALEY

MODEL	SPARK PLUGS		CYL. HEAD NUTS		CON. ROD BOLTS		MAIN BRG. NUTS		MANIFOLDS		ROCKER ARM SHAFT BRKTS.		FLYWHEEL TO CRANKSHAFT BOLTS	
	Ft. Lbs.	M. Kg.	Ft. Lbs.	M. Kg.	Ft. Lbs.	M. Kg.	Ft. Lbs.	M. Kg.	Ft. Lbs.	M. Kg.	Ft. Lbs.	M. Kg.	Ft. Lbs.	M. Kg.
AUSTIN:														
A40, A2S6	30	4.0	40	5.5	35	4.8	60	8.3					40	5.5
A55	30	4.0	40	5.5	35	4.8	70	9.7					35	4.8
A60	30	4.0	40	5.5	35	4.8	70	9.7	15	2.1	25	3.4	35	4.8
850	30	4.0	40	5.5	33	4.5	65	9.0			25	3.5	110	15.2
AUSTIN-HEALEY:														
BN1, BN2	30	4.0	65	8.9									35	4.8
BN4, BN6, BN7, BT7, BJ7, & BJ8	30	4.0	75	10.4	50	6.9	75	10.4			25	3.5	50	6.9
Sprite Mk I, II, & III	27	3.7	40	5.5	35	4.8	60	8.3	15	2.1	25	3.4	40	5.5

of the cylinder is below the peg and the spring is compressed. Withdraw the wrench and insert the plunger assembly into the body. Replace the back plate and secure the assembly to the cylinder block.

When the timing chain is in position, the tensioner is released for operation by inserting the wrench and turning it clockwise until the slipper head moves forward against the timing chain under spring pressure. *CAUTION: Do not force the slipper into the chain.* Secure the bolts with the lock plate and replace the bottom plug. Lock it with the tab washer.

PISTON AND ROD ASSEMBLY

There is some variation in assembly instructions; therefore, this information is listed under each car model.

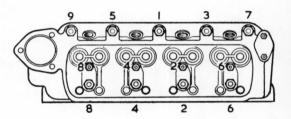

Cylinder head bolt tightening sequence.

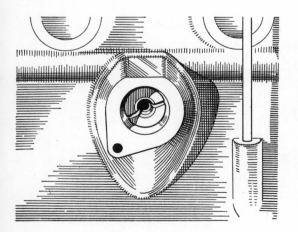

The large offset in the distributor drive flange must face up when No. 1 piston is at TDC firing position.

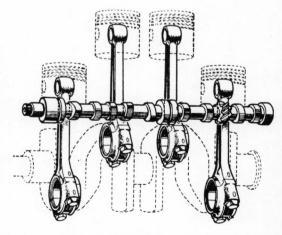

When correctly assembled and installed in the engine, each rod offset side faces away from a main bearing.

MECHANICAL ENGINE SPECIFICATIONS—AUSTIN, AUSTIN-HEALEY

MODEL	BORE		CRANKSHAFT						PISTON PIN					
			Con. Rod Journal		Main Brg. Journal		End Play		Diameter		Fit in Rod F = Free P = Interference		Fit in Piston F = Free P = Interference	
	In.	Mm.	In.	Mm.	In.	Mm.	In.	Mm.	In.	Mm.	In.	Mm.	In.	Mm.
AUSTIN:														
A40, A2S6	2.4778-2.4781	62.935-62.940	1.6254-1.6259	41.285-41.298	1.7505-1.7510	44.463-44.475			.6244-.6246	15.860-15.865	Clamped	Clamped	.0001P-.0003F	.0025P-.0076F
A55	2.8757-2.8760	73.043-73.050	1.8759-1.8764	47.648-47.661	2.0005-2.0010	50.813-50.825	.002-.003	.051-.076	.6869-.6871	17.447-17.452	Clamped	Clamped	.0001-.00035F	.0025-.0090F
A60	3.0011-3.0014	76.227-76.235	1.8759-1.8764	47.648-47.661	2.0005-2.0010	50.813-50.825	.002-.003	.051-.076	.6869-.6871	17.447-17.452	.0001-.0006F Clamped	.0025-.0150F Clamped	.0001-.00035F	.0025-.009F
850	2.4778-2.4781	62.935-62.940	1.6254-1.6259	41.285-41.298	1.7505-1.7510	44.463-44.475	.002-.003	.051-.076	.5620	14.27	Clamped	Clamped	.0001-.00035F	.0025-.0090F
AUSTIN-HEALEY:														
BN1, BN2	3.4375	87.3	2.0000-2.0005	50.800-50.812	2.4790-2.4795	62.966-62.979	.002-.003	.0508-.0762	.8748-.8750	22.219-22.225	Clamped	Clamped	.0001-.00035F	.0025-.0090F
BN4, BN6	3.1245-3.126	79.362-79.4	2.0000-2.0005	50.80-50.8127	2.3742-2.3747	60.305-60.317	.0025-.0055	.063-.140	.8748-.8750	22.215-22.220	Clamped	Clamped	.0004F	.01016F
BN7 & BT7	3.2805-3.282	83.32-83.36	2.0000-2.0005	50.80-50.8127	2.3742-2.3747	60.305-60.317	.0025-.0055	.063-.140	.8748-.8750	22.215-22.220	.0001-.0006F	.0025-.0150F	.0004F	.01016F
BJ7 & BJ8	3.2805-3.282	83.32-83.36	2.0000-2.0005	50.80-50.8127	2.3742-2.3747	60.305-60.317	.0025-.0055	.063-.140	.8748-.8750	22.215-22.220	.0001-.0006F	.0025-.0150F	.0004F	.01016F

MECHANICAL ENGINE SPECIFICATIONS—AUSTIN, AUSTIN-HEALEY

MODEL	BORE In.	BORE Mm.	Con. Rod Journal In.	Con. Rod Journal Mm.	Main Brg. Journal In.	Main Brg. Journal Mm.	End Play In.	End Play Mm.	Diameter In.	Diameter Mm.	PISTON PIN Fit in Rod In. F = Free P = Interference	Fit in Rod Mm.	Fit in Piston In. F = Free P = Interference	Fit in Piston Mm.
Sprite Mk I 948 cc	2.4778-2.4781	62.935-62.940									Clamped	Clamped	.0001P-.0003F	.00254P-.0076F
Sprite Mk II 948 cc			1.6254-1.6259	41.285-41.298	1.7505-1.7510	44.463-44.475	.002-.003	.051-.076	.6244-.6246	15.86-15.865	Clamped	Clamped	.0001-.00035F	.0025-.009F
Sprite Mk II 1098 cc	2.5420-2.5435	64.567-64.605	1.6254-1.6259	41.285-41.298	1.7505-1.7510	44.463-44.475	.002-.003	.051-.076	.6244-.6246	15.86-15.865	.0001-.0006F	.0025-.0150F	.0001-.00035F	.0025-.009F
Sprite Mk III 1098 cc	2.5420-2.5435	64.567-64.605					.002-.003	.051-.076	.6244-.6246	15.86-15.865	.0001-.0006F	.0025-.0150F	.0001-.00035F	.0025-.009F

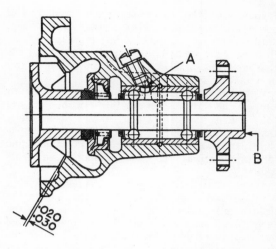

Cross section of the water pump. The hole (A) must align with the lubricating hole in the body. The face of the hub (B) must be flush with the end of the spindle.

ENGINE NOTES—AUSTIN-HEALEY 100/3,000

PISTON AND ROD ASSEMBLY

Assemble the piston to the rod so that the slit in the piston skirt is on the same side as the slit (or bolt side) of the connecting rod. The piston is installed in the engine so that the slit in the piston faces away from the camshaft. The big ends of the connecting rods are offset; rods numbered 1, 3, and 5 towards the front, and 2, 4 and 6 towards the rear. From engine No. 40501, the piston pin clamp bolt was replaced by a full floating pin. Make sure that the slit in the piston faces opposite the camshaft when installing. *NOTE: On the BN 1 & BN 2 models only, the piston pin clamp bolts alternate between sides.*

ENGINE REMOVAL

The engine can be removed with or without the transmission.

Remove the radiator, and then take off the fan assembly. Disconnect the throttle linkage at the firewall. Disconnect the choke control cable and remove the air cleaners. Disconnect the fuel line at the common fuel inlet. Turn off the battery master switch located inside of the luggage compartment. Remove the ignition high-tension cables. Disconnect the wire to the distributor and remove the distributor. Disconnect the heater hoses from the engine. Disconnect the generator and coil low-tension cables, and move the harness to one side. Remove the generator and coil assembly. Take off the oil filter and disconnect the oil pressure flexible pipe at its upper end. Remove the starting motor. Take out the four bolts holding each engine mount to the frame. Unscrew the six brass nuts holding the exhaust pipe to the manifolds and lower the pipe.

Remove the valve rocker arm shaft assembly and attach a lifting fixture. Place a strain on the chain until the mounting brackets just leave the frame. Remove the four bolts holding the right-hand engine mounting bracket to the cylinder block, and then take off the mounting bracket.

WITHOUT THE TRANSMISSION. Use a jack to support the transmission and take out the nuts and bolts holding the bell housing to the block. Hoist the engine to provide clearance between the crankshaft damper and the crossmember. Pull the engine forward to release the clutch from the mainshaft splines.

WITH THE TRANSMISSION. Remove the seat cushions, and then take out the clips holding the padded arm rest to the central tunnel. Roll the carpet back over the short tunnel to expose the twelve screws holding the tunnel to the body of the car. Remove the screws, the tunnel, and the carpeting. Remove six screws and take off the carpet-covered bulkhead. Remove the propeller shaft flange bolts. Take out the four bolts from the transmission mounting brackets. Remove the speedometer cable. Remove the bolts holding the stabilizer bar to the frame. Detach the clutch slave cylinder from the bell housing. *NOTE: The slave cylinder push rod is released from the clutch operating lever by removing the clevis pin.* Hoist the engine and transmission assembly from the engine compartment.

ENGINE SERVICE NOTES—SPRITE

PISTON AND ROD ASSEMBLY

Make sure that the groove of the pin lines up with the hole in the rod before inserting the locking bolt. The solid-skirted pistons should be marked before disassembly. When installed in the engine, the piston pin clamp bolt must be on the camshaft side of the engine.

ENGINE REMOVAL

The engine can be removed with or without the transmission.

GENERAL. Disconnect the ground cable from the battery. Remove the hood from its hinges. Disconnect the heater hoses and remove the radiator. Disconnect the choke and throttle cables, the oil pressure gauge pipe, the tachometer cable, and all low-tension cables. Remove the high-tension wires from the spark plugs and at the coil, and then remove the distributor cap. Disconnect the starter cable and the fuel lines. Release the clamp holding the exhaust pipe to the manifold and lower it out of the way.

REMOVING THE ENGINE WITH THE TRANSMISSION. Remove the cover around the gearshift lever. Take out the antirattle cap, spring, and plunger. Remove the gear change lever retaining plate setscrews and take off the retaining plate and lever assembly. Turn back the carpet and remove the transmission rear mounting bolts. From underneath the car, remove the speedometer cable and release the clip holding it to the bell housing. Detach the slave cylinder from the bell housing by taking out the bolts and withdrawing the push rod from the rear of the cylinder. Disconnect the propeller shaft from the rear axle and remove it from the vehicle over the left-hand side of the differential case. Remove the remaining transmission mounting bolts and lift out the engine with a chain hoist.

REMOVING THE ENGINE WITHOUT THE TRANSMISSION. Remove the filter bowl and the starting motor. Support the transmission with a jack and remove the bolts holding the transmission to the engine. Remove the left-hand engine mount rubber together with the front exhaust pipe support bracket from the bell housing. Use a chain hoist to lift the engine from the frame.

RACING MODIFICATIONS—SPRITE

The standard engine develops 43 Bhp @ 5,200 rpm and this can be extended to 54 Bhp if certain modifications are made. For example, lightly polishing the intake and exhaust ports and matching up the manifold ports with the cylinder head ports will generally give about 2 additional hp. Grinding out the intake manifold to 1⅛″ diameter throughout is also effective.

Two additional Hp can be obtained by installing special 9.3/1 compression ratio pistons (Part No. 2A.946) and resetting the ignition timing to 3° BTDC.

50 Bhp can be obtained by installing a new camshaft (Part No. 2A.948), valve springs (2A.950), carburetor needles (GG with air cleaners or GM without air cleaners), and distributor (2A.951). The ignition timing should be set to 1° BTDC and 93/97 octane rating gasoline used.

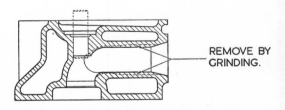

REMOVE BY GRINDING.

Fig. 2. Section through the inlet port.

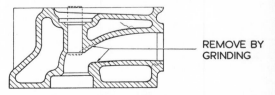

REMOVE BY GRINDING

Fig. 3. Section through the exhaust port.

Modification of the Sprite intake manifold (see text).

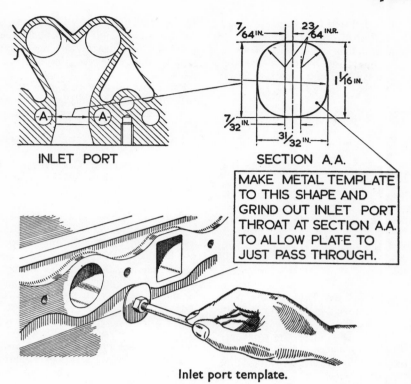

INLET PORT

SECTION A.A.

MAKE METAL TEMPLATE
TO THIS SHAPE AND
GRIND OUT INLET PORT
THROAT AT SECTION A.A.
TO ALLOW PLATE TO
JUST PASS THROUGH.

Inlet port template.

Racing modifications for the Sprite (see text).

An additional 2 hp can be obtained by altering the shape of the intake and exhaust ports as shown in Fig. 2 and 3 of the accompanying illustrations. Make a sheet metal template as shown and fasten it to a long bolt to check your work carefully as the resulting wall between the push rod holes will be 0.086″ thick *only if properly centered.* If off-center, you may go through the wall. Grind out the exhaust ports as shown in Fig. 3. Be sure to use GG or GM carburetor needles as indicated above.

A special tuned exhaust system is available which will give an additional 2 to 3 hp.

Additional Points

With the special racing camshaft, valve bounce will occur at 6,300 to 6,400 rpm. This can be raised to 6,700 rpm by adding an outer spring (Part No. 2A950) and an extra inner spring (Part No. AEA401). New bottom and top spring collars (Part No. AEA402 & AEA432) must be fitted for this condition. To fit the bottom collar, it will be necessary to spot face the small cast recesses on top of the cylinder head around the valve guides to a diameter of 0.875″ for the collars to seat squarely. The depth of the facing should be ³⁄₃₂″ below the outer valve spring face. The valve bounce position can be further raised to 7,000 rpm by using the standard outer valve spring (Part No. AEA311).

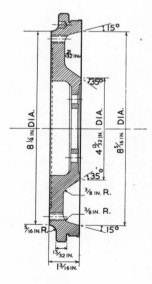

Fig. 4

Sectioned Sprite flywheel to show where lightening can be accomplished and the finished dimensions.

The flywheel can be lightened as shown in Fig. 4. Be sure to rebalance it after machining.

For strengthening the engine, if it is to be used exclusively for racing purposes, special parts are available as follows: a stronger crankshaft, exhaust valves, clutch, transmission, and rear end.

ENGINE NOTES—AUSTIN A40

ENGINE REMOVAL

The engine and transmission can be removed as a unit, or the engine can be removed without the transmission.

FROM INSIDE OF THE ENGINE COMPARTMENT. Drain the cooling system. Remove the battery and radiator. Disconnect the exhaust pipe at the manifold flange and the support bracket from the bell housing. Disconnect the fuel line, throttle linkage, and the wiring to the starter, generator, and coil. Disconnect the oil pressure indicator switch, and the ground strap.

FROM INSIDE OF THE CAR. Remove the four screws holding the transmission cover plate and lift out the gear shift lever.

FROM UNDER THE CAR. Disconnect the speedometer cable. Support the transmission with a jack. If it is to be removed with the engine, disconnect the transmission from the crossmember. If the transmission is to remain, remove the bell housing bolts.

FROM INSIDE OF THE ENGINE COMPARTMENT. Attach a sling so that the engine can be pulled to a nearly vertical position in order to clear the front crossmember. Remove the nut and washer holding the two front engine mounts to the brackets, and then remove one of the brackets from the frame to allow enough freedom of engine movement. Lift the engine up and forwards.

PISTON AND ROD ASSEMBLY

The rods are offset and, therefore, must be replaced properly as marked. Rods numbered 1 and 3 are offset towards the front of the engine, while numbers 2 and 4 are offset towards the rear. Assemble the piston to the rod so that the slit in the piston skirt is on the same side as the slit at the top of the connecting rod. When installed in the engine, the slit in the piston skirt and the slit at the top of the connecting rod must face the camshaft.

ENGINE NOTES—AUSTIN A55

ENGINE REMOVAL

The engine and transmission must be removed as a unit, or the entire front suspension system can be removed with the power plant. The front suspension system can be released from the body by removing the four nuts and rubber washers at the front and rear of the suspension assembly.

FROM THE ENGINE COMPARTMENT. Remove the hood, battery, battery tray, and the radiator. Drain the oil from the engine and transmission. Disconnect

the heater hoses, the oil pressure pipe, and the starting motor cable. Disconnect the wires to the generator, coil, distributor, and water temperature sending unit. Release the exhaust pipe at the manifold.

FROM INSIDE OF THE CAR. Remove the rubber dust cover from the shift lever, release the lock ring, and withdraw the shift lever. If the car has a steering column shift lever, remove the selector control rod and the shift rod from their levers on the transmission.

FROM UNDER THE CAR. Remove the clevis pin from the clutch slave cylinder push rod and remove the slave cylinder. *NOTE: Do not disconnect the cylinder but tie it out of the way.* Disconnect the speedometer cable and remove the propeller shaft.

FROM INSIDE OF THE ENGINE COMPARTMENT. Attach a lifting tackle and support the engine weight. Loosen the two rear, one front, and one side engine mounts. Take off the two nuts on the inner face of each mount so that the engine mounts can be moved slightly to permit separation from the engine.

FROM UNDER THE CAR. Position a jack under the transmission to support the weight, and then remove the rear crossmember. Take off the engine steady rest from its rubber mount at the transmission and the bolts holding the transmission rubber mounts to the crossmember. The jack can now be removed, but it is advisable to have a helper steady the rear end of the power plant to keep it from scraping the floor as it must be withdrawn at a sharp angle.

OIL PAN REMOVAL

Drain the oil, remove the 19 bolts, and then lower the oil pan.

PISTON AND ROD ASSEMBLY

The top of the piston is marked FRONT, and the piston pin clamp screw must face the camshaft (left) side of the engine.

ENGINE SERVICE NOTES—AUSTIN 850

ENGINE REMOVAL

FROM INSIDE OF THE CAR. Take out the hexagon plug and remove the antirattle spring and plunger from the gear shift extension. Remove the two bolts holding the gear shift lever retaining plate, and pull out the lever. Disconnect the ground lead to the battery.

FROM UNDER THE HOOD. Remove the hood at the hinges. Disconnect the heater inlet and exhaust hoses. Remove the carburetor. Disconnect the wires from the oil pressure warning light, stop light switch, coil, generator, and distributor. Remove the distributor cap complete with all high-tension wiring. Remove the cable from the starting motor and from the clip on the subframe. Remove the ground cable from the clutch cover. Disconnect

WINDSHIELD WIPER MOTOR

CARBURETORS

RADIATOR

HEATER CONTROL

GENERATOR   FAN

The Austin 850 has the engine mounted crosswise in the front of the car. The transmission and differential units are in the oil pan.

the speedometer cable from the rear of the speedometer. Disconnect the hydraulic brake supply pipe at the three-way union on the engine fire wall and plug the pipe with a clean 3/8" SAE bolt to keep the system from draining. Remove the entire exhaust system. Support the body with a suitable

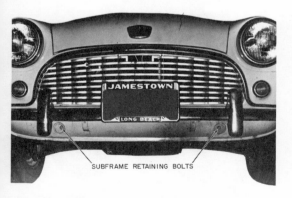

SUBFRAME RETAINING BOLTS

To remove the power plant and front subframe assembly, two bolts must be removed through the front bumper.

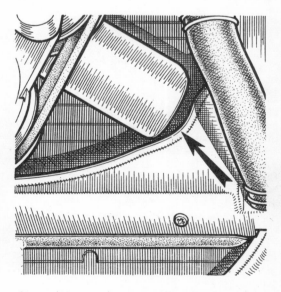

The radiator cowling is notched to assist in removing the fan belt. Turn the fan blade to this position to remove the belt.

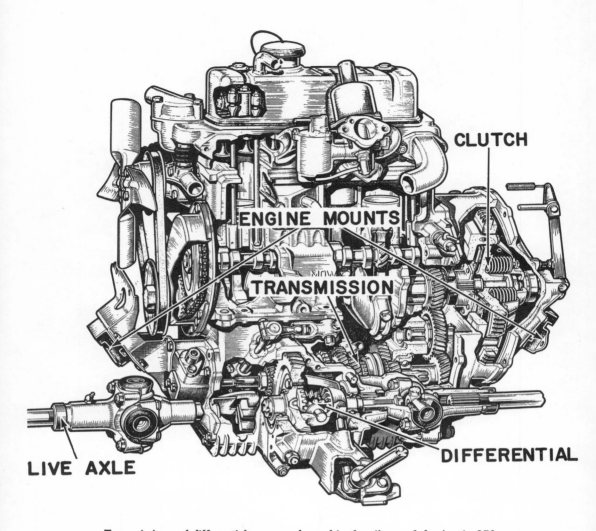

CLUTCH

ENGINE MOUNTS

TRANSMISSION

LIVE AXLE

DIFFERENTIAL

Transmission and differential gears are housed in the oil pan of the Austin 850.

sling underneath each front fender. Take out the two bolts holding the slave cylinder to the flywheel housing, release the lever tension spring, pull the push rod from the cylinder, and wire the unit against the engine firewall. Disconnect the steering rack ball ends from the steering levers and remove the telescopic dampers. Release the engine tie-rod from its bracket at the rear of the cylinder block. Support the engine from under the transmission. Take out the four body-to-subframe bolts, two on each side of the firewall crossmember.

FROM UNDER THE CAR. Take out the four bolts holding the rear of the subframe to the front floor and the two bolts holding the front of the frame to the bottom of the grille panel. Lift the body clear of the engine and pull out the subframe and engine assembly. Care should be taken when lifting the body to avoid damage to the radiator and cowling.

After disconnecting the power plant, the body must be raised to release the power plant and subframe assembly.

The drive is through the front wheels on the Austin 850. This highly-tuned model with two carburetors is called the Austin Mini-Cooper.

MINI-COOPER SPECIFICATIONS

The Austin Mini-Cooper is a special highly-tuned model with a larger engine than is installed in the Austin 850. This car has been imported with three different engines, the smallest being 59.1 cu. in. (970 cc.). This engine had a compression ratio of 9.75/1.0 and developed 65 hp at 6,500 rpm. The bore was 2.781″ (70.64 mm.) and the stroke 2.4365″ (61.91 mm.).

The next larger engine to make its appearance in this car was the 1100 engine, 65.35 cu. in. (1071 cc.). This engine came with a compression ratio of 9.0/1.0 and developed 68 hp at 5,750 rpm. The bore was 2.781″ (70.64 mm.) and the stroke 2.687″ (68.26 mm.).

The present engine is the 1300, 77.9 cu. in. (1275 cc.). This engine has a compression ratio of 9.5/1.0 and develops 75 hp at 5,800 rpm. The bore is 2.781″ (70.64 mm.) and the stroke 3.20″ (81.33 mm.).

The fuel system consists of two HS-2 S.U. carburetors. The other mechanical details are the same as the present 1071 cc. engine.

The engine can be lifted from the subframe after disconnecting the drive mechanism.

6

Clutch, Transmission, and Differential

CLUTCH

The clutch is a single-plate, dry-disc type mounted on the flywheel. A steel cover, bolted to the flywheel, encloses the driven plate, the pressure plate, the springs, and the release fingers. The driven plate has a splined hub, which is mounted on the clutch shaft to drive the transmission pinion.

The throw-out mechanism is hydraulically actuated. When the clutch pedal is depressed, fluid pressure is transmitted through the master cylinder to the slave cylinder, which is mounted on the clutch housing. This moves the slave cylinder piston and push rod, which is connected to the throw-out lever. The push rod is not adjustable. If the system is disconnected, it must be bled to remove air.

BLEEDING THE CLUTCH SYSTEM

Remove the bleed screw dust cap at the slave cylinder, open the bleed screw ¾ turn, and attach a tube, immersing the open end in a clean receptacle containing a small amount of brake fluid. Fill the

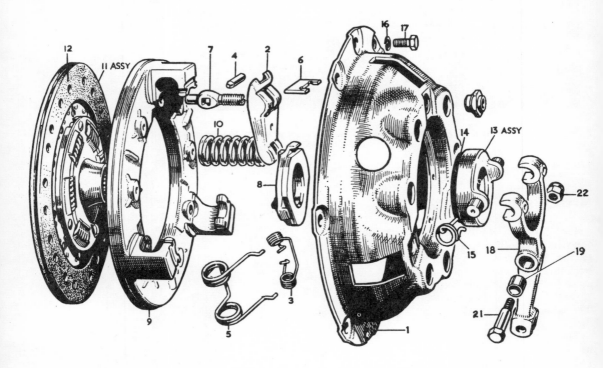

Details of the clutch used on all BMC cars: (1) cover—clutch, (2) lever—release, (3) retainer—lever, (4) pin—lever, (5) spring—anti-rattle, (6) strut, (7) eyebolt with nut, (8) plate—bearing thrust, (9) plate—pressure, (10) spring—pressure plate, (11) plate assembly—driven, (12) lining, (13) ring assembly—thrust, (14) carbon, thrust bearing, (15) retainer, (16) washer—spring—cover screw, (17) screw—cover-to-flywheel, (18) lever—withdrawal, (19) bushing, (21) bolt for lever, (22) nut for bolt. To service the clutch and/or transmission, the entire power plant must be pulled on the Austin A55, Austin A60, and the Sprite. The clutch and/or transmission can be removed without pulling the engine on the Austin A40 and all Austin-Healey models.

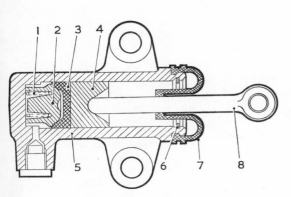

Cross-sectioned view of the slave cylinder used on the Sprite.

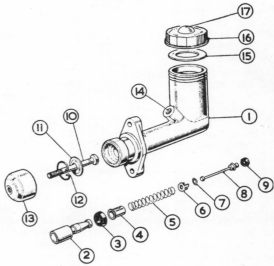

master cylinder reservoir with brake fluid, depress the clutch pedal, close the bleed screw, and allow the pedal to return. Continue this series of operations until the fluid in the container is free of air bubbles.

OVERHAULING A BMC TRANSMISSION

DESCRIPTION

These transmissions are basically alike because they all have four-forward speeds, synchronized in the top three speeds. Some models of the Austin-Healey and M. G. are equipped with an overdrive unit. Some of the smaller cars use bushings in place of needle bearings between the mainshaft and gears. In addition, the Austin-Healey has a detachable bell housing.

DISASSEMBLING

① Some models have an overdrive unit which must be detached before the transmission can be disassembled. To do this, remove the transmission cover and the six bolts holding the overdrive unit to the transmission adapter plate. *CAUTION: Because the overdrive unit contains strong springs, it is necessary to release the pressure gradually. To do this, remove the four nuts on the short studs,*

1. Master cylinder body.	10. Push-rod.
2. Plunger.	11. Retaining washer.
3. Plunger seal.	12. Circlip.
4. Spring thimble.	13. Dust cover.
5. Spring.	14. Outlet.
6. Valve spacer.	15. Cap washer.
7. Spring washer.	16. Filler cap.
8. Valve stem.	17. Air vent.
9. Valve seal.	

The clutch throw-out mechanism is hydraulically operated in other models and has no free play adjustment. This exploded view shows the details of the clutch master cylinder.

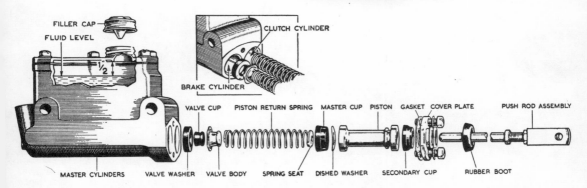

The Sprite clutch and brake master cylinder. Note that no valve is used in the clutch cylinder.

No.	Description	No.	Description	No.	Description
1.	Case assembly.	31.	Thrust washer (rear).	61.	Screw.
2.	Stud for front cover.	32.	Third motion shaft.	62.	Spring washer.
3.	Stud for side cover.	33.	Third and fourth speed synchronizer.	63.	Reverse wheel with bush.
4.	Dowel.	34.	Ball.	64.	Bush.
5.	Filler plug.	35.	Spring.	65.	Reverse fork.
6.	Drain plug.	36.	Sleeve.	66.	Reverse fork rod.
7.	Plug for reverse plunger spring.	37.	Third speed gear with cone.	67.	First and second speed fork.
8.	Washer.	38.	Synchronizing cone.	68.	First and second speed fork rod.
9.	Front cover.	39.	Needle roller.	69.	Third and fourth speed fork.
10.	Front cover joint.	40.	Third speed gear locking collar.	70.	Third and fourth speed fork rod.
11.	Spring washer.	41.	Second speed gear with cone.	71.	Fork locating screw.
12.	Nut.	42.	Synchronizing cone.	72.	Shakeproof washer.
13.	Side cover.	43.	Needle roller.	73.	Nut.
14.	Joint for side cover.	44.	Second speed locking collar.	74.	Interlock plunger.
15.	Spring washer.	45.	Collars.	75.	Interlock ball.
16.	Nut.	46.	Peg for locking collar.	76.	Plug.
17.	First motion shaft with cone.	47.	Spring for peg.	77.	Washer.
18.	Synchronizing cone.	48.	First speed gear assembly.	78.	Plunger for fork rod.
19.	Needle-roller bearing.	49.	Ball.	79.	Spring.
20.	First motion shaft journal ball bearing.	50.	Spring for ball.	80.	Clutch withdrawal lever with bush.
21.	Spring ring.	51.	Third motion shaft journal ball bearing.	81.	Bush.
22.	Washer.	52.	Bearing housing.	82.	Bolt.
23.	Lock washer.	53.	Spring ring.	83.	Spring washer.
24.	Nut.	54.	Bearing packing washer.	84.	Locking washer.
25.	Layshaft.	55.	Third motion shaft distance piece.	85.	Nut.
26.	Laygear.	56.	Speedometer gear.	86.	Dust cover.
27.	Needle-roller bearing with spring ring.	57.	Plain washer.	87.	Dust cover for bell housing.
28.	Distance piece.	58.	Locking washer.	88.	Starter pinion cover.
29.	Spring ring.	59.	Third motion shaft nut.	89.	Screw.
30.	Thrust washer (front).	60.	Reverse shaft.	90.	Washer.

Sprite transmission nomenclature.

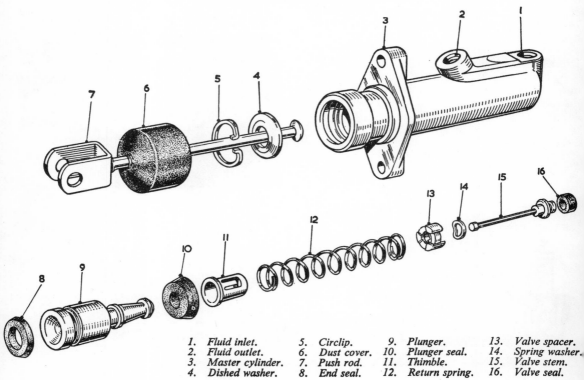

1.	Fluid inlet.	5.	Circlip.	9.	Plunger.	13.	Valve spacer.
2.	Fluid outlet.	6.	Dust cover.	10.	Plunger seal.	14.	Spring washer.
3.	Master cylinder.	7.	Push rod.	11.	Thimble.	15.	Valve stem.
4.	Dished washer.	8.	End seal.	12.	Return spring.	16.	Valve seal.

Exploded view of the clutch and brake master cylinders used on the Austin-Healey.

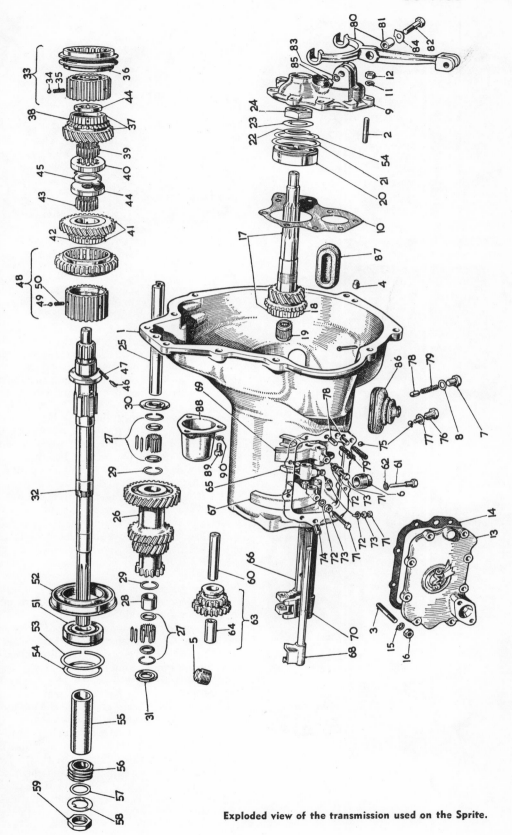

Exploded view of the transmission used on the Sprite.

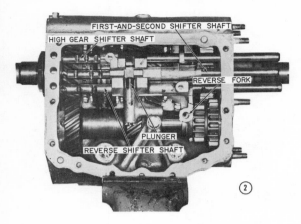

(2)

Labels on image: FIRST-AND-SECOND SHIFTER SHAFT, HIGH GEAR SHIFTER SHAFT, REVERSE FORK, PLUNGER, REVERSE SHIFTER SHAFT

(3)

Labels on image: CLUTCH SHAFT, MAINSHAFT, CLUSTER GEAR, REVERSE IDLER, RETAINER BOLT

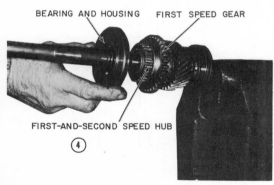

(4)

Labels on image: BEARING AND HOUSING, FIRST SPEED GEAR, FIRST-AND-SECOND SPEED HUB

(5)

Labels on image: SYNCHRONIZER SLEEVE

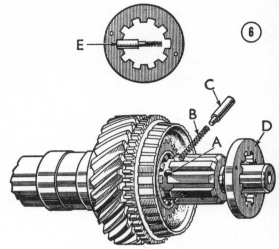

(6)

Labels on image: E, C, B, A, D

and then remove the two nuts on the long studs, turning them evenly until the pressure is released. Pull the overdrive unit from the adapter plate. The overdrive pump cam should slide freely along the mainshaft providing access to the lock ring holding the spacer to the rear adapter plate. Remove the lock ring and slide the spacer from the shaft. Pull the adapter plate from the transmission. Remove the clutch bell housing and the shift lever remote control unit, if the transmission has no overdrive.

② Remove the fork retaining bolts, and then remove the shafts and forks in the following order: (1) the reverse shaft and fork, together with its selector and detent plungers and springs, (2) the high-gear shifter shaft, (3) the first-and-second shifter shaft and fork, and (4) the high-gear fork. *CAUTION: Be careful not to drop the two interlock balls which are located one on each side of the center shifter shaft.*

③ Remove the reverse shaft retaining bolt, push out the shaft, and lift the reverse idler gear from the case. Tap out the countershaft and allow the cluster gear to drop to the bottom of the case. Withdraw the clutch shaft from the front and the mainshaft assembly from the rear. Lift out the cluster gear and thrust washers.

④ From the rear of the mainshaft, remove the retaining nut, lock washer, speedometer drive gear, bearing, and housing. Slide the first-speed gear, with the first-and-second speed hub, from the shaft. *CAUTION: Be careful not to drop the balls and springs located in the first-speed gear hub.*

⑤ From the forward end, slide the synchronizer sleeve and two balk rings from the shaft.

⑥ Depress the plunger holding the third-speed gear lock plate (D), rotate the plate to line up the splines, and then slip it from the shaft. Remove the plunger (C) and spring (B), and then slide the third-speed gear and its 32 rollers from the shaft. Depress the second-speed gear collar locking plunger and then rotate the collar to line up the splines.

The teeth of the cluster gear wear.

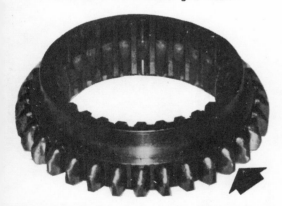

The teeth of the synchronizer hub round off like this.

The reverse idle gear wears in this manner.

The synchronizing cone of the clutch gear wears in this manner.

Slide the collar from the shaft, remove the two halves of the washer holding the spring and plunger, and then remove the second-speed gear and roller bearings, if so equipped.

CLEANING AND INSPECTING

Clean all parts in solvent and blow dry. Do not spin the ball bearings with compressed air, or they will be damaged. After a thorough cleaning, lubricate the bearings with light oil to prevent rusting. Turn the lubricated bearings slowly through your fingers to feel for roughness and excess play.

Inspect the case for cracks or burrs which might hinder the seating of a snap ring. Dress off any burrs with a fine-cut mill file.

The tapered surface of the synchronizer cones should be inspected for this damage.

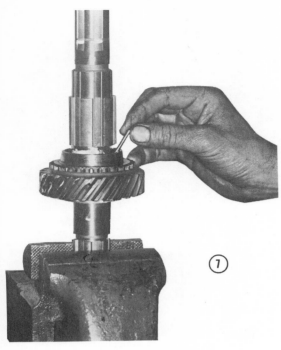

(7)

Check the gear teeth for spalling, the bushings for wear, the needle bearings for pits, the thrust washers for damage, and the synchronizing cones for wear.

ASSEMBLING

(7) Lubricate the mainshaft, and then install the second-speed gear with the synchronizer cone facing towards the rear of the transmission. Install the 33 needle bearings, if so equipped.

(8) Replace the spring and the locking plunger. Install the two halves of the second-speed gear washer.

(9) Slide the collar onto the splines, depress the locking plunger with a sharp tool, and push the collar into position, locating the lugs of the washer in the cut-outs of the collar. Rotate the collar to move the splines out of line.

(10) Invert the mainshaft in the vise, and then slide the bearing race over the splines. Lubricate the parts and install the third-speed gear. Replace the 32 needle bearings, if so equipped.

(11) Replace the spring and the locking plunger. Slide the locking plate over the splines, depress the plunger with a sharp instrument, and then rotate the plate to move the splines out of line.

(12) Insert the springs and balls into the holes of the synchronizer hub, and then assemble the shifting sleeve over it with both balk rings to lock the assembly in position. Assemble the first-and-second speed hub, slide the assembly over the mainshaft, and then install the speedometer drive gear,

(8)

(9)

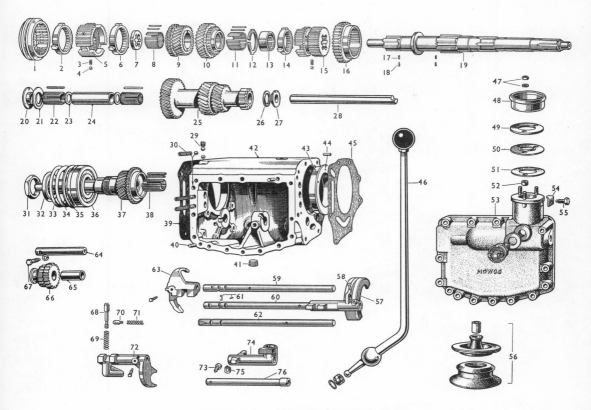

Exploded view of the BMC transmission.

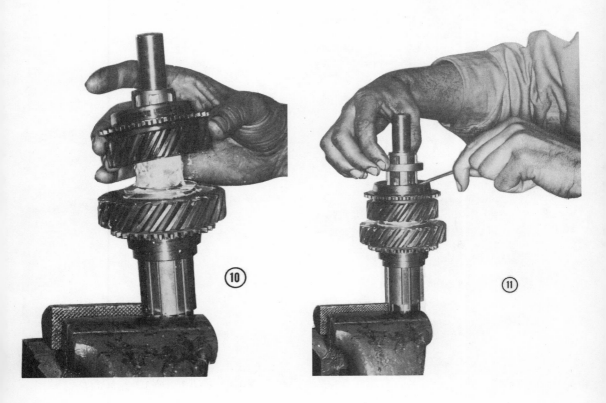

(12)

THIRD-AND-FOURTH SHIFTER FORK — FIRST-AND-SECOND SHIFTER FORK

SELECTOR PLUNGER — REVERSE FORK

(16)

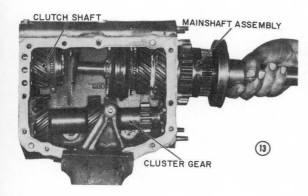

CLUTCH SHAFT — MAINSHAFT ASSEMBLY

CLUSTER GEAR

(13)

the bearing, and the retainer to complete the mainshaft assembly.

(13) Assemble the cluster gear over a dummy shaft. Replace the needle bearings at each end, separated by the spacer. Hold the needle bearings in position with grease. Position the thrust washer at each end of the gear, slide the assembly into the transmission case, and allow it to rest on the bottom. Replace the clutch shaft assembly, with the 16 needle bearings held in position with grease. Insert the mainshaft assembly from the rear of the case. *CAUTION: Be careful not to dislodge the needle bearings in the clutch shaft as the mainshaft moves into the clutch shaft bearing.*

(14) Lift the cluster gear into position while fitting the thrust washer locks into the grooves provided. Slide the countershaft through the housing and gear

(14)

SHAFT

SETSCREW HOLE — REVERSE IDLER GEAR

(15)

INTERLOCK — THIRD-AND-FOURTH GEAR SHIFTER SHAFT

FIRST-AND-SECOND GEAR SHIFTER SHAFT

(17)

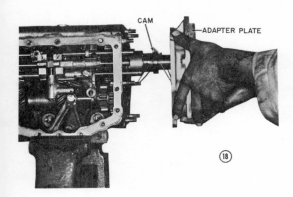

which pushes the dummy shaft from the other end. The cut-away portion of the countershaft must be aligned to fit the groove in the bell housing, which keeps the countershaft from turning.

⑮ Replace the reverse idler gear, slide the shaft through it, and then tighten the setscrew.

⑯ Slip the third-and-fourth speed shifter fork into position, followed by the first-and-second speed shifter fork, and then the reverse fork and shaft, with its selector and detent plungers and springs.

⑰ Replace one interlock ball above the first-and-second speed shifter shaft, and then slide the third-and-fourth speed shifter shaft into position. Insert the remaining interlock ball, holding it with grease. Replace the fork setscrews, and then lock them with wire.

Removing the clutch housing of the Austin 850.

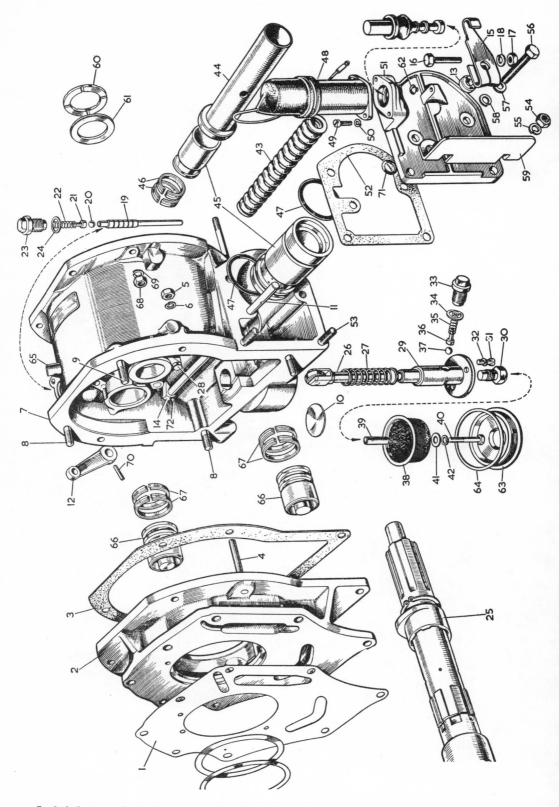

Exploded view of the front case of a Laylock de Normanville overdrive unit used on the Austin-Healey.

Components of overdrive front casing.

1. Joint washer.
2. Adaptor plate.
3. Joint washer.
4. Locating stud.
5. Nut.
6. Spring washer.
7. Main casing.
8. Stud.
9. Stud.
10. Welch plug.
11. Valve operating shaft.
12. Setting lever.
13. Collar.
14. Shaft cam.
15. Solenoid lever.
16. Adjusting screw.
17. Nut.
18. Washer.

19. Valve push rod.
20. Ball valve.
21. Ball valve plunger.
22. Valve spring.
23. Valve plug.
24. Copper washer.
25. Third motion shaft.
26. Pump plunger.
27. Plunger spring.
28. Guide peg.
29. Pump body.
30. Pump body plug.
31. Body screw.
32. Spring washer.
33. Valve plug.
34. Plug washer.
35. Valve spring.
36. Ball valve plunger.

37. Ball valve.
38. Pump filter.
39. Distance piece.
40. Filter bolt.
41. Plain washer.
42. Spring washer.
43. Accumulator spring.
44. Distance tube.
45. Piston assembly.
46. Piston rings.
47. Rubber rings.
48. Solenoid unit.
49. Unit screw.
50. Spring washer.
51. Solenoid lever housing.
52. Joint washer.
53. Stud.
54. Nut

55. Spring washer.
56. Setpin.
57. Plain washer.
58. Spring washer.
59. Solenoid shield.
60. Thrust washer.
61. Spacing washer.
62. Rubber stop.
63. Drain plug.
64. Drain plug washer.
65. Breather.
66. Piston.
67. Piston rings.
68. Nut.
69. Spring washer.
70. Cotter pin.
71. Oil seal.
72. Peg.

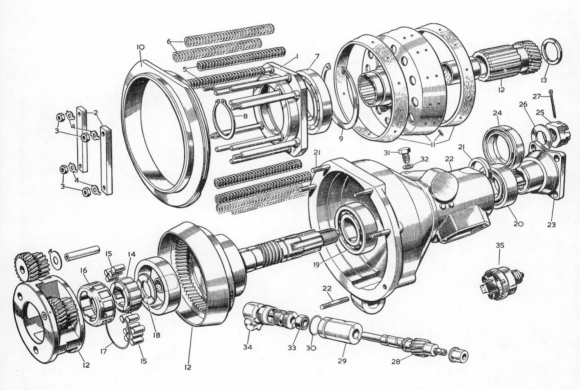

1. Clutch thrust ring.
2. Bridge pieces.
3. Nuts.
4. Locking washers.
5. Clutch spring (long).
6. Clutch spring (short).
7. Front bearing.
8. Circlip (small).
9. Circlip (large).

10. Brake ring.
11. Clutch assembly.
12. Sun wheel assembly.
13. Thrust washer.
14. Uni-directional clutch.
15. Rollers.
16. Outer casing.
17. Securing clip.
18. Thrust washer.

19. Inner bearing.
20. Outer bearing.
22. Rear housing.
21. Spacing washer.
23. Driving flange.
24. Oil seal.
25. Flange nut.
26. Washer.
27. Split pin.

28. Speedometer spindle.
29. Spindle sleeve.
30. Washer.
31. Locking peg.
32. Washer.
33. Oil seal.
34. Spindle adaptor.
35. Overdrive switch.

Exploded view of the rear case of the overdrive.

⑱ Bolt the rear extension in position. *NOTE: The plain bearing plate is placed against the bearing.* For models with. an overdrive, install the adapter plate and tighten the eight bolts holding the plate to the transmission. Replace the clutch bell housing and the side cover. For models without an overdrive, replace the shift lever remote control unit.

TRANSMISSION SERVICE—AUSTIN 850

These automobiles have the transmission in the engine oil pan with the differential gears coming out of the side of the pan. The engine is mounted crosswise in the chassis, and the drive is through the front wheels.

The transmission and/or differential can be serviced after removing the engine and subframe assembly as described in the chapter on engines.

FLYWHEEL AND CLUTCH
ASSEMBLY REMOVAL

The clutch can be removed without removing the engine. Disconnect the wires from the coil and remove it from the flywheel housing. Remove the starter. Take out the clevis pin from the clutch operating lever, release the tension spring, pull the

push rod from the slave cylinder, and remove the lever assembly from the clutch cover. Take out the slave cylinder mounting screws and wire the unit to the engine firewall. Remove the exhaust pipe clamp and the radiator cowling steady bracket. Remove the two nuts and bolts holding the engine mounts to the subframe side member, and then take out the nine bolts holding the clutch cover to the flywheel housing. Raise the engine only enough to remove the cover. *CAUTION: Make sure that the fan blades do not strike the radiator core.* Take out the three nuts and remove the clutch thrust plate from the pressure spring housing. *CAUTION: It is essential that No. 1 cylinder be positioned at TDC before removing the flywheel.* It is only in this position that the "C" washer, which locates the primary gear, cannot drop. Unless this precaution is taken, the washer can drop behind the flywheel and become wedged in the oil seal, damaging it seriously. Release the locking washer and loosen the flywheel retaining screw three or four threads. Use a puller to break the flywheel from the taper seat on the crankshaft. *CAUTION: The bolts used to hold the puller to the flywheel must not have over ½" (12.70 mm.) threaded length; otherwise, they will protrude through the flywheel*

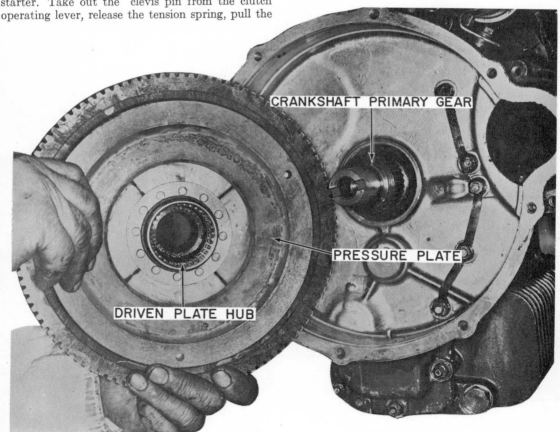

CRANKSHAFT PRIMARY GEAR

PRESSURE PLATE

DRIVEN PLATE HUB

The clutch driven and pressure plates are located behind the flywheel.

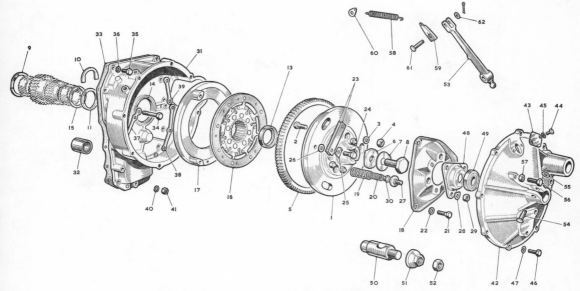

Exploded view of the flywheel and clutch assembly.

and damage the clutch driven plate. Remove the flywheel retaining screw and the keyed driving washer. Withdraw the flywheel and clutch as an assembly. *NOTE: A rubber plug is installed in the rear end of the crankshaft as a precaution against oil leaking past the brass taper plug. If there is evidence of oil leakage at this point, remove the plug, drive the brass tapered plug firmly into the oil gallery, and install a new rubber sealing plug.*

OVERHAULING THE TRANSMISSION AND DIFFERENTIAL ASSEMBLY

Transmission Removal. After the engine and subframe assembly is removed from the body, as explained in the engine chapter, remove the flywheel and clutch assembly. Take off the starting motor. Take out the 12 bolts from the flange of the transmission case, noting the length of each screw for assembly purposes.

Differential Removal. Take off the hexagon cap, and remove the shift lever antirattle spring and plunger from the shift lever extension. Take out the four bolts and remove the bottom cover plate from the extension. Remove the clamp bolts holding the link to the top of the remote control shaft, release the link, and withdraw the shaft. Remove the nylon seating-and-tension spring from both the operating shaft and the link. Take out the nuts holding the right- and left-hand driving flanges to the differential gear shafts and withdraw the flanges. Take out the five bolts from each of the final drive end covers and lift off the covers. Note the number of shims installed between the differential bearing and the housing. Remove the

differential housing nuts and withdraw the housing from the case. Remove the differential assembly.

Transmission Disassembly. Remove the idler gear from the crankcase. Note the thrust washers on each side of the gear. Take out the detent plunger plug and remove the spring and plunger. Take out the clamp screw and lift off the shift

This is the "C" washer discussed in the text.

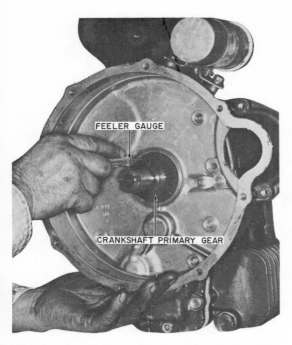

A feeler gauge blade is handy for easing the lip of the seal into position when installing the flywheel cover.

lever. Remove the speedometer pinion gear and housing. Remove the nine bolts and take off the transmission end cover. Remove the bolts holding the oil suction pipe, and then slip the pipe from the filter. Remove the plate holding the third gear shaft bearing retainer to the center web of the case, and then remove the retainer shims. Take out the third gear shaft drive pinion nut, lock washer, and the drive pinion. Remove the lock ring and roller bearing from the end of the first

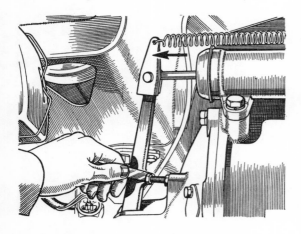

The clutch lever must be adjusted so that a clearance of 0.045" (1.143 mm.) exists between the operating lever and the stop.

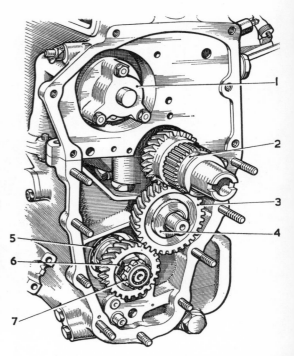

This shows the gearing arrangement with the flywheel housing removed. (1) Oil pump, (2) crankshaft primary gear, (3) idler gear, (4) idler gear thrust washer, (5) transmission drive gear bearing, (6) transmission drive gear, (7) roller bearing.

gear shaft, take off the nut, and lift the first gear shaft driving gear from the case. Remove the clustergear and reverse gear shaft locking plates, push the clustergear shaft from the case, and remove the clustergear and thrust washers. Remove the retainer plugs from the outside of the case, and then lift out the selector rod interlocking plungers and spring. Remove the first gear shaft bearing lock ring. Use a punch to remove the bearing from the case. Unlock the first-and-second speed selector fork, withdraw the rod, and lift the fork from the case. Remove the third gear shaft bearing by moving the shaft forward to free the bearing from the center web. After removing the bearing, lift the shaft from the case. Remove the remaining oil strainer bracket screw and lift out the strainer. Release the locknut and setscrew holding the third-and-fourth gear selector fork, and then slide the rod out to release the fork. Remove the reverse gear shaft, gear, and selector fork, and then remove the detent spring and plunger. Release the lock ring from the reverse gear shift lever pivot pin and remove the lever.

DIFFERENTIAL DISASSEMBLY. Remove the two differential bearings. Remove the six bolts holding the driving gear to the cage. Mark the gear and cage to assist in assembly. Separate the gear from the cage and remove the differential gear and thrust washer from the bore of the driving gear. Tap out the tapered pin to release both the pinions and thrust washers, pinion spacer, and the other differential gear and washer. The tapered pin cannot be removed until the cage and driving gear are separated.

DIFFERENTIAL ASSEMBLY AND ADJUSTMENTS. Assembly is the reverse of disassembly. Make sure that the differential gear thrust washers are installed with their chamfered bores against the machined faces of the differential gears. Install the differential into the transmission case, slightly angled toward the flywheel end of the engine. Install the differential housing with its gasket, tightening the nuts snugly but not too tight. Install the right-hand cover with its gasket, making sure that the holes in the cover and the tapped hole in the case and differential housing line up. Tighten the bolts evenly. Install the left-hand drive cover *without its gasket*. Tighten the cover only enough to make firm contact with the bearing outer race. *CAUTION: Overtightening will distort the cover flange.* Use a feeler gauge to measure the distance between the cover flange and the differential housing as shown at A in the accompanying illustration. This measurement should be made at several positions. Variation in measurement will indicate that the flange has been distorted by uneven tightening.

Installing the differential gears.

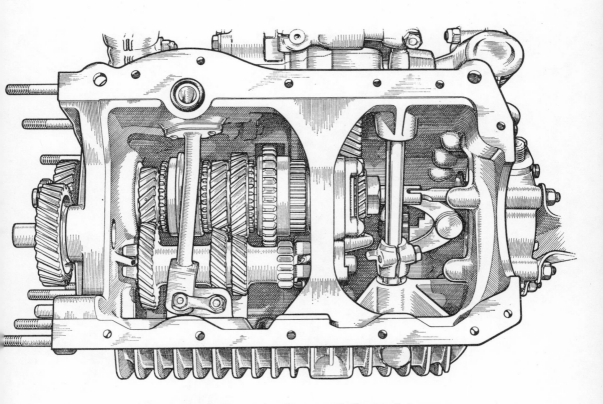

This is the oil pan, showing the placement of all transmission gears.

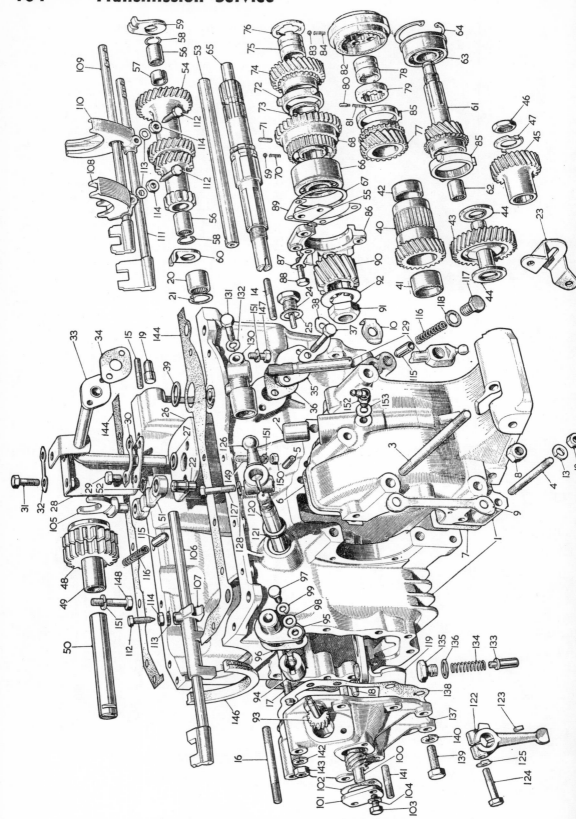

Exploded view of the gears for the Austin 850.

No.	Description	No.	Description	No.	Description
1.	Transmission case.	53.	Layshaft.	104.	Washer.
2.	Control shaft bush.	54.	Laygear.	105.	Reverse fork.
3.	Differential cover stud.	55.	Locating plate.	106.	Reverse fork rod.
4.	Differential cover stud.	56.	Bearing.	107.	Fork rod selector.
5.	Differential cover dowel.	57.	Distance piece.	108.	First and second speed fork.
6.	Differential cover joint washer (upper).	58.	Retaining ring.	109.	First and second speed fork rod.
7.	Differential cover joint washer (lower).	59.	Thrust washer (rear).	110.	Third and fourth speed fork.
8.	Differential cover stud nut.	60.	Thrust washer (front).	111.	Third and fourth speed fork rod.
9.	Washer.	61.	First motion shaft.	112.	Selector screw.
10.	Washer.	62.	First motion shaft roller bearing.	113.	Washer.
12.	Differential cover stud nut.	63.	First motion ball bearing.	114.	Locknut.
13.	Washer.	64.	Circlip.	115.	Plunger fork end.
14.	Flywheel housing stud.	65.	Third motion shaft.	116.	Plunger spring.
15.	Flywheel housing stud.	66.	Third motion shaft bearing.	117.	Plug.
16.	Front cover stud (long).	67.	Circlip.	118.	Plug washer.
17.	Front cover stud (short).	68.	First speed gear.	119.	Change speed gate.
18.	Front cover dowel.	69.	Synchronizer ball.	120.	Gear change shaft.
19.	Flywheel housing dowel.	70.	Spring.	121.	Oil seal.
20	Idler gear bearing.	71.	Second speed synchronizer plunger.	122.	Operating lever.
21.	Bearing circlip.	72.	Baulk ring.	123.	Key.
22.	Operating lever pin.	73.	Second speed gear thrust washer.	124.	Lever screw.
23.	Exhaust pipe bracket.	74.	Second speed gear.	125.	Washer.
24.	Drain plug.	75.	Bush.	126.	Change shaft lever.
25.	Plug washer.	76.	Interlocking ring.	127.	Lever screw.
26.	Oil strainer.	77.	Third speed gear.	128.	Washer.
27.	Sealing ring.	78.	Bush.	129.	Remote-control shaft.
28.	Strainer bracket.	79.	Third motion shaft thrust washer.	130.	Shaft lever.
29.	Screw to strainer.	80.	Thrust washer peg.	131.	Lever screw.
30.	Washer.	81.	Spring.	132.	Washer.
31.	Screw to casing.	82.	Third/top synchronizer.	133.	Reverse check plunger.
32.	Washer.	83.	Ball.	134.	Plunger spring.
33.	Oil suction pipe.	84.	Spring.	135.	Spring plug.
34.	Joint washer.	85.	Baulk ring.	136.	Plug washer.
35.	Pipe flange.	86.	Bearing retainer.	137.	Front cover.
36.	Joint washer.	87.	Lock washer.	138.	Cover joint.
37.	Pipe screw.	88.	Screw.	139.	Cover screw.
38.	Washer.	89.	Bearing shim.	140.	Washer.
39.	Sealing ring.	90.	Final drive pinion.	141.	Mounting adaptor stud.
40.	Primary gear.	91.	Nut.	142.	Washer.
41.	Gear bush (front).	92.	Washer.	143.	Nut.
42.	Gear bush (rear).	93.	Speedometer pinion.	144.	Crankcase joint washer—R.H.
43.	Idler gear.	94.	Bush.	145.	Crankcase joint washer—L.H.
44.	Idler gear thrust washer.	95.	Bush assembly.	146.	Bearing cap oil seal.
45.	First motion shaft gear.	96.	Joint washer.	147.	Transmission to crankcase screw.
46.	Nut.	97.	Bush screw.	148.	Transmission to crankcase screw (long).
47.	Lock washer.	98.	Washer.	149.	Transmission to crankcase stud.
48.	Reverse gear.	99.	Washer.	150.	Nut.
49.	Bush.	100.	Speedometer spindle and gear.	151.	Washer.
50.	Reverse shaft.	101.	End plate.	152.	Lubricator differential cover.
51.	Reverse operating lever.	102.	Plate joint.	153.	Lubricator differential cover washer.
52.	Pivot pin circlip.	103.	Screw.		

Transmission nomenclature.

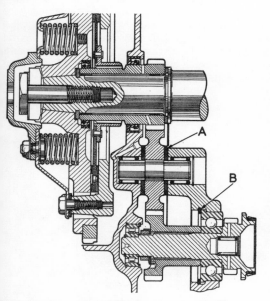

Cross section through the idler gear and the clutch shaft. The idler gear must have 0.003"–0.008" (0.076–0.20 mm.) end play at "A" and is adjustable by replacing the lock ring at "B" with one that is of a different thickness.

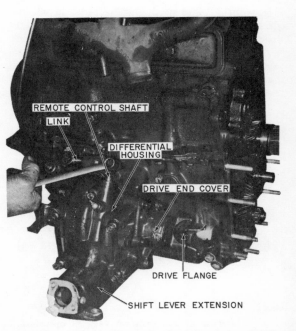

The differential housing is on the side of the oil pan.

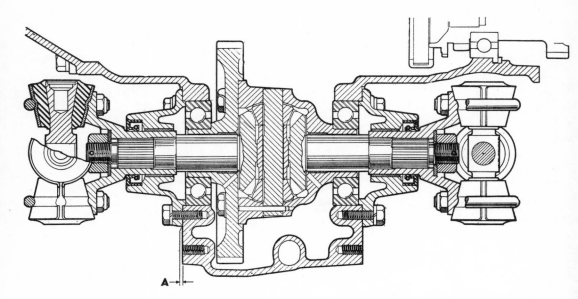

Method of obtaining the differential bearing preload as discussed in the text. The measurement at "A" must be made without a gasket in place.

The compressed thickness of the cover gasket is 0.007″ (0.178 mm.) and the required preload on the bearings is 0.001″ to 0.002″ (0.025 to 0.051 mm.). The measured gap should, therefore, be 0.008″ to 0.009″ (0.203 to 0.229 mm.). Any deviation from this figure must be made up by shimming. Remove the end cover and install a new gasket and the required shims. Tighten the cover screws evenly. Tighten the differential housing nuts, install the driving flanges to the differential gear shafts, and lock them in position with the nuts and cotter pins. *CAUTION: Make sure that the driveshafts are equally free to rotate, as tightness of either one will cause the car to pull to one side.* The rest of the assembly is the reverse of disassembly.

REAR AXLE

The rear axle is the familiar three-quarter floating type using hypoid gears. The axle shafts and the pinion and differential assembly can be withdrawn without removing the rear axle assembly from the vehicle. The rear wheel bearing assemblies are located in the hubs, and the inner races are mounted on the axle tubes and held in place by means of a nut and lockwasher. The differential and pinion shaft bearings are preloaded, the amount of preload being adjusted by shims. The backlash between the pinion and ring gear is adjustable by shims.

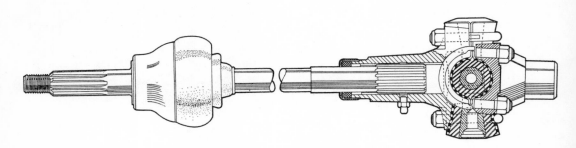

Details of the constant-velocity universal joints used on the Austin 850. They cannot be repaired and must be replaced when worn.

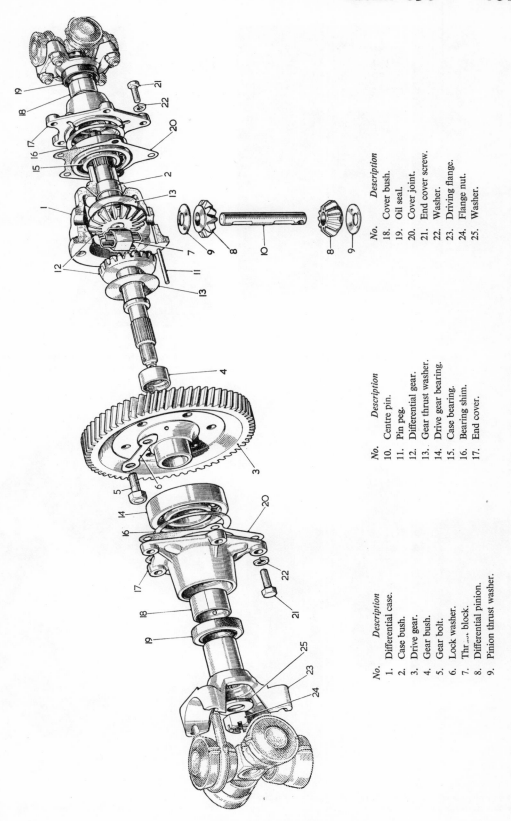

The differential components of the Austin 850.

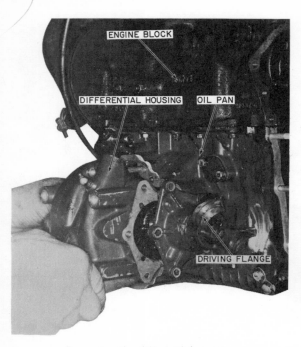

Removing the differential cover.

To lubricate the constant-velocity universal joints the covers must be removed by untwisting the retaining wires.

The rubber bushings of the universal joints deteriorate in this manner and must be replaced to eliminate play.

The new rubber bushings are retained by "U" clamps.

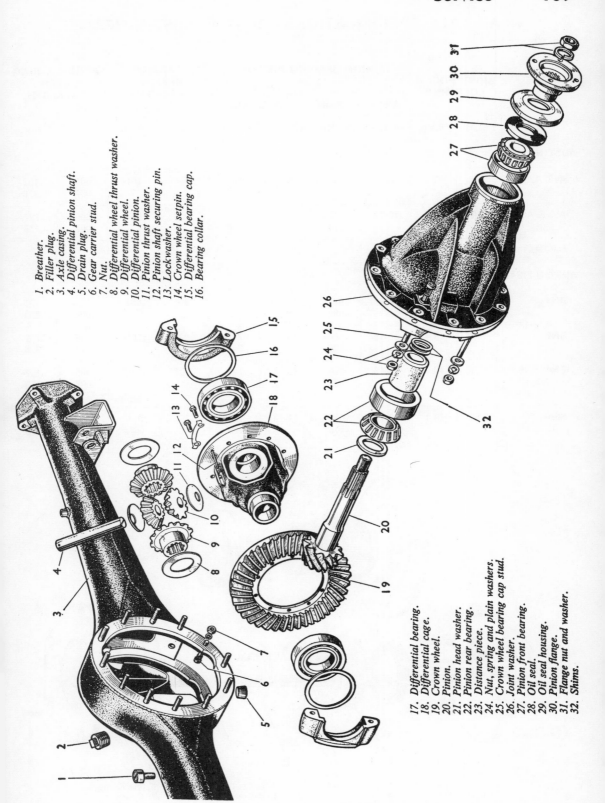

1. Breather.
2. Filler plug.
3. Axle casing.
4. Differential pinion shaft.
5. Drain plug.
6. Gear carrier stud.
7. Nut.
8. Differential wheel thrust washer.
9. Differential wheel.
10. Differential pinion.
11. Pinion thrust washer.
12. Pinion shaft securing pin.
13. Lockwasher.
14. Crown wheel setpin.
15. Differential bearing cap.
16. Bearing collar.

17. Differential bearing.
18. Differential cage.
19. Crown wheel.
20. Pinion.
21. Pinion head washer.
22. Pinion rear bearing.
23. Distance piece.
24. Nut, spring and plain washers.
25. Crown wheel bearing cap stud.
26. Joint washer.
27. Pinion front bearing.
28. Oil seal.
29. Oil seal housing.
30. Pinion flange.
31. Flange nut and washer.
32. Shims.

Exploded view of a typical BMC rear axle assembly.

REAR AXLE SPECIFICATIONS—AUSTIN, AUSTIN-HEALEY

MODEL	DRIVE PINION LOCK NUT		PINION BEARING PRELOAD				CARRIER BEARING PRELOAD		PINION & RING GEAR BACKLASH	
			Without Oil Seals		With Oil Seals					
	Ft.Lbs.	M.Kg.	In. Lbs.	M. Kg.	In. Lbs.	M. Kg.	In.	Mm.	In.	Mm.
AUSTIN:										
A40, A2S6	140	19.4	8-10	.092-.115	9-13	.104-.149	.004	.1016	.004-.007	.102-.178
A55 & A60	140	19.4	10-12	.12-.14	13-15	.149-.173	.002	.051	.005-.007	.127-.178
850 See text										
AUSTIN-HEALEY:										
BN1	140	19.4	6-8	.07-.092			.002	.051	.005-.008	.127-.203
BN2	140	19.4	16-18	.184-.207	19-21	.219-.242	.004	.1016	.006-.012	.152-.306
BN4, BN6, BN7, BT7, BJ7, & BJ8	140	19.4	16-18	.184-.207	13-15	.149-.173	.004	.1016	.005-.007	.127-.178
Sprite Mk I, II, & III	140	19.4	8-10	.092-.115	11-13	.126-.149	.002	.051	.004-.007	.102-.178

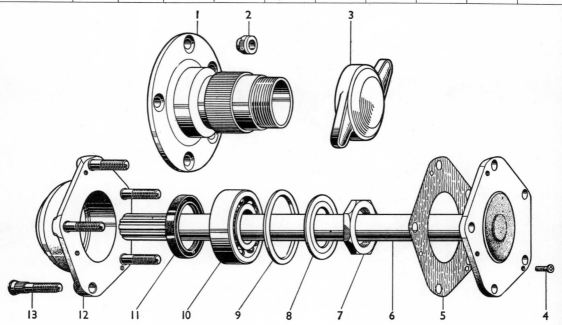

1. Hub extension.
2. Securing nut.
3. Hub cap.
4. Securing screw.
5. Joint washer.
6. Half shaft.
7. Hub locknut.
8. Hub lockwasher.
9. Bearing spacer.
10. Hub bearing.
11. Oil seal.
12. Hub casing.
13. Hub extension stud.

Details of the Austin-Healey rear axle.

7

Running Gear

WHEEL SUSPENSION

Most models use the familiar wishbone type, independent front wheel suspension with coil spring for the front and with leaf springs for the rear.

WHEEL ALIGNMENT

Toe-in is the only front wheel angle that can be adjusted in BMC cars. The specifications for the other front end angles are given in the specification table so that bent parts can be located and replaced to re-establish the correct front end alignment.

The steering gear adjustment (arrow) should be turned down until all free play is removed with the wheels in the straight-ahead position, but not enough to cause a bind when turning the wheel.

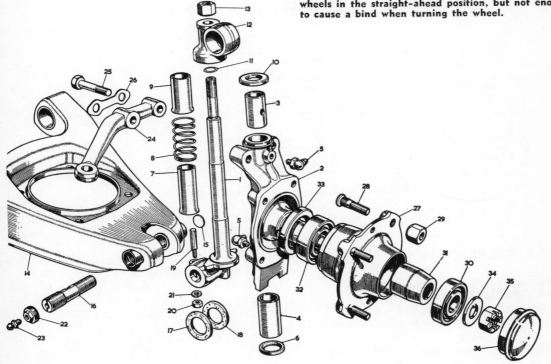

Details of the Sprite front suspension.

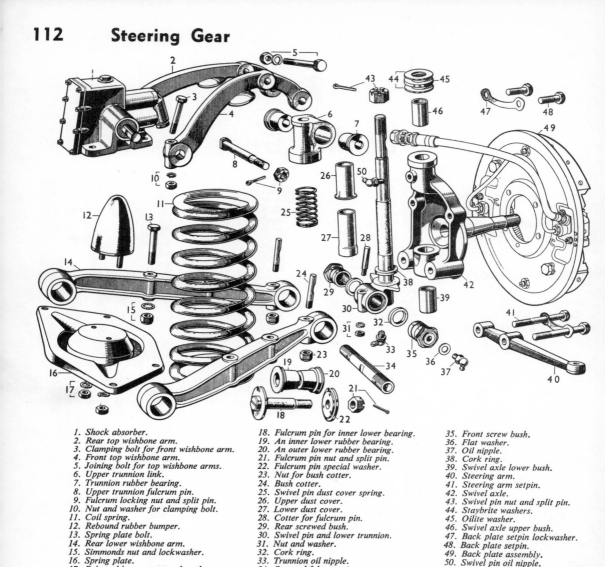

1. Shock absorber.
2. Rear top wishbone arm.
3. Clamping bolt for front wishbone arm.
4. Front top wishbone arm.
5. Joining bolt for top wishbone arms.
6. Upper trunnion link.
7. Trunnion rubber bearing.
8. Upper trunnion fulcrum pin.
9. Fulcrum locking nut and split pin.
10. Nut and washer for clamping bolt.
11. Coil spring.
12. Rebound rubber bumper.
13. Spring plate bolt.
14. Rear lower wishbone arm.
15. Simmonds nut and lockwasher.
16. Spring plate.
17. Rebound bumper nut and washer.

18. Fulcrum pin for inner lower bearing.
19. An inner lower rubber bearing.
20. An outer lower rubber bearing.
21. Fulcrum pin nut and split pin.
22. Fulcrum pin special washer.
23. Nut for bush cotter.
24. Bush cotter.
25. Swivel pin dust cover spring.
26. Upper dust cover.
27. Lower dust cover.
28. Cotter for fulcrum pin.
29. Rear screwed bush.
30. Swivel pin and lower trunnion.
31. Nut and washer.
32. Cork ring.
33. Trunnion oil nipple.
34. Screwed fulcrum pin.

35. Front screw bush.
36. Flat washer.
37. Oil nipple.
38. Cork ring.
39. Swivel axle lower bush.
40. Steering arm.
41. Steering arm setpin.
42. Swivel axle.
43. Swivel pin nut and split pin.
44. Staybrite washers.
45. Oilite washer.
46. Swivel pin upper bush.
47. Back plate setpin lockwasher.
48. Back plate setpin.
49. Back plate assembly.
50. Swivel pin oil nipple.

Details of the Austin-Healey front suspension.

FRONT HUB ADJUSTMENT

The front hub end play adjustment is made by inserting or removing shims from between the outer bearing and the spacer. Install the assembly as shown in the illustration, without any shims, and tighten the nut while rotating the hub to seat the bearings parts. Remove the nut, washer, and the outer bearing cone. Insert a sufficient number of shims to produce an excessive amount of end play. Replace the bearing cone, washer, and the nut. Measure the end play, and then remove just enough shims to eliminate all play while still allowing the hub to rotate freely. The nut should be tightened to 40–70 ft.-lbs. torque (5.53–9.68 mkg.). Latitude in this reading is given for alignment of the cotter key hole.

STEERING GEAR ADJUSTMENTS—RACK AND PINION

The end play of the pinion shaft must be between 0.002" and 0.005" (0.05 and 0.13 mm.). It is adjusted by adding or removing shims. A rack damper adjustment must be made to keep the rack moving through the housing with minimum play. To make this adjustment, remove the damper, spring, and shims. Replace the plunger in the cap and screw the assembly into position until it is just possible to rotate the pinion shaft by drawing the rack through the housing. Now measure the distance between the hexagon of the plunger cap and its seat on the housing. Shims should be inserted between the cap and rack which total 0.002" to 0.005" (0.05 to 0.13 mm.) more than the measured clearance without the shim pack or spring. Shims are available in 0.003" (0.08 mm.) thickness.

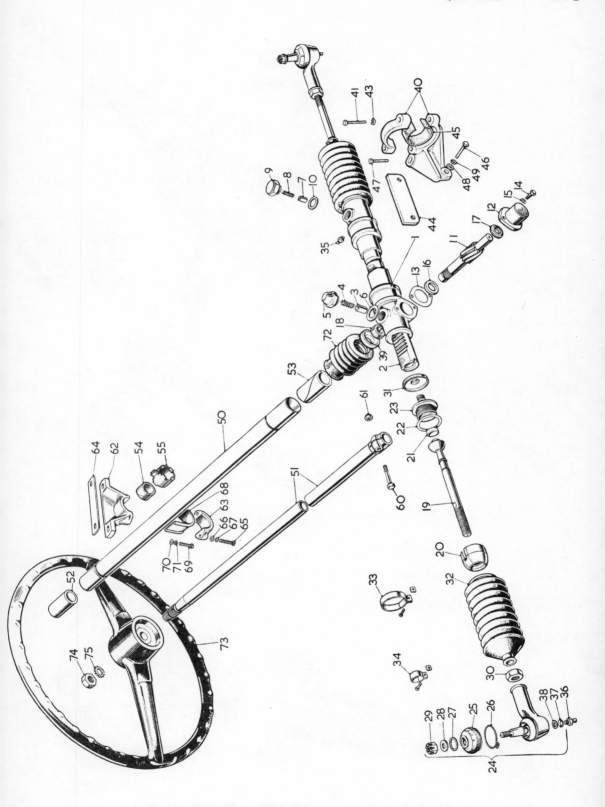

Exploded view of the steering gear mechanism used on the Sprite.

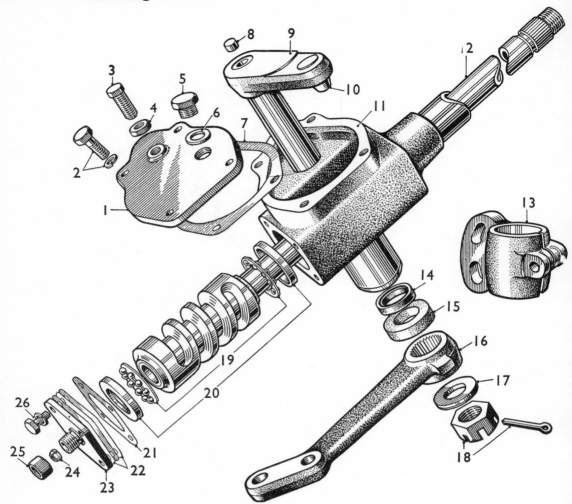

Exploded view of the steering gear mechanism used on the Austin and Austin-Healey.

1. *Grease cup.*
2. *Axle nut.*
3. *Split pin.*
4. *Washer.*
5. *Outer bearing.*
6. *Bearing outer race.*
7. *Hub.*
8. *Bearing outer race.*
9. *Inner bearing.*
10. *Oil seal.*
11. *Brake disc.*

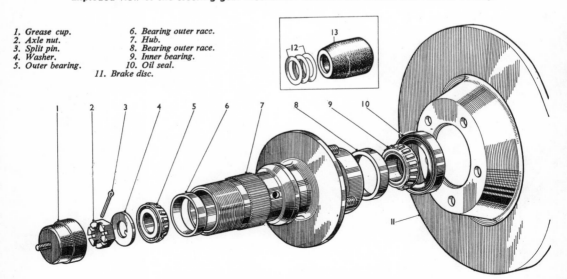

Exploded view of the Austin-Healey front hub, which must rotate with zero end play. The adjusting shims and spacers are shown in the inset.

WHEEL ALIGNMENT SPECIFICATIONS—AUSTIN, AUSTIN-HEALEY

MODEL	CASTER (Degrees)① P=Positive	CAMBER (Degrees)① N=Negative	STEERING AXIS INCLINATION (Degrees)	TOE-IN		TOE OUT ON TURNS (Degrees)	
				In.	Mm.	Inner Wheel	Outer Wheel
AUSTIN:							
A40	P3	P½	6½	1/16-1/8	1.59-3.18	24¾	20
A55	P1½	P1	6½	0-1/8	0-3.18	24¾	20
A55 Mk II	P3	P¾	6½	Nil	Nil	24¾	20
A60	P1½	P¾	6½	1/16-1/8	1.58-3.17	24	20
850	P3	P1②	9½	1/16②③	1.59	25	20
AUSTIN-HEALEY:							
All	P2	P1	6½	1/16-1/8	1.58-3.17	24¼	20
Sprite Mk I, II & III	P3	P1	6½	0-1/8	0-3.18	24¾	20

① Caster and camber are not adjustable.
② Rear wheel camber P1°, toe-in ⅛″ (3.18 mm.).
③ The front wheels are toed out.

BRAKES

Two types of braking systems are used on BMC cars; drum and disc types. The drum brakes contain a single wheel cylinder. Its piston forces one shoe into contact with the drum, and the reaction pushes the cylinder back along a slot in the backing plate to move the other shoe into contact with the drum. In other words, a single piston is used to do the work of two.

Most of the newer models use disc brakes on the front and drum type brakes on the rear wheels.

Some of the lighter models use a pressure regulating valve in the lines to the rear brakes to limit the hydraulic pressure that can be applied to the rear wheels.

DRUM TYPE BRAKE ADJUSTMENTS

FRONT WHEELS. Remove the access hole rubber plugs in the wheel disc, and then rotate the brake drum until both adjustment screws are visible in the two holes of the brake drum. Turn each screw clockwise until the wheel locks, and then back off each adjuster one notch at a time until the wheel is free.

REAR WHEELS. The same procedure applies for the rear wheel brakes, except that only one hole and one adjuster is used to position both rear shoes and also the hand brake at the same time. The wheel cylinder floats on the backing plate and operates both shoes.

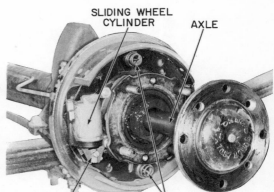

SLIDING WHEEL CYLINDER   AXLE

MICRAM ADJUSTER RETAINING SPRING

Rear rear brake details.

The brake shoes can be adjusted by removing the wheel and turning the "Micram" adjusters through a hole in the drum.

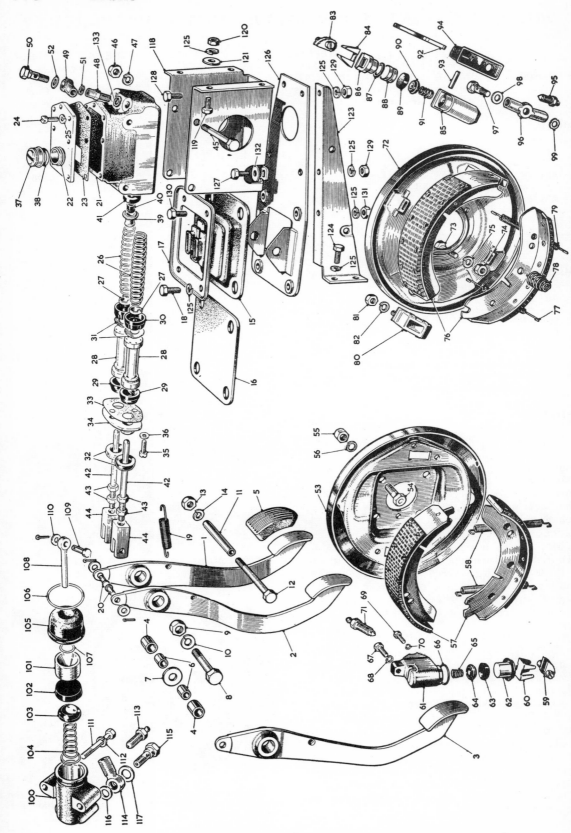

Parts of the front and rear wheel cylinders used on the early Sprite models. Later models used disc brakes on the front wheels.

No.	Description	No.	Description	No.	Description
1.	Brake pedal.	45.	Bolt—master cylinder to box.	89.	Cup—piston.
2.	Clutch pedal—right-hand drive.	46.	Nut—master cylinder to box bolt.	90.	Filler cup.
3.	Clutch pedal—left-hand drive.	47.	Washer—spring.	91.	Spring—filler.
4.	Bush.	48.	Adaptor—master cylinder.	92.	Lever—hand brake.
5.	Rubber pad—pedal.	49.	Banjo—master cylinder.	93.	Pin—lever.
6.	Distance-piece—pedal.	50.	Bolt—banjo.	94.	Boot—hydraulic cylinder.
7.	Distance washer—pedal.	51.	Gasket—banjo connection.	95.	Screw—bleeder.
8.	Bolt—pedal bracket.	52.	Gasket—banjo connection.	96.	Banjo connection—wheel cylinder.
9.	Nut—pedal bracket bolt.	53.	Plate—L/H front brake.	97.	Bolt—banjo connection.
10.	Washer—spring.	54.	Bolt—brake back-plate.	98.	Gasket—banjo connection—large.
11.	Distance tube—pedal stop.	55.	Nut—brake back-plate.	99.	Gasket—banjo connection—small.
12.	Distance tube—bolt.	56.	Washer—spring—brake back-plate.	100.	Body.
13.	Nut—distance tube bolt.	57.	Shoe—lined—brake.	101.	Piston.
14.	Spring washer.	58.	Spring—shoe pull-off.	102.	Cup—piston.
15.	Fume excluder—brake and clutch pedal.	59.	Adjuster.	103.	Filler—piston cup.
16.	Rubber—blanking piece.	60.	Mask—adjuster.	104.	Spring—cup filler.
17.	Cover—blanking piece.	61.	Body—L/H.	105.	Boot.
18.	Cover screw.	62.	Piston and dust cover.	106.	Clip—large—boot.
19.	Spring—pedal pull-off.	63.	Cup—piston.	107.	Clip—small—boot.
20.	Clevis pin.	64.	Filler—piston cap.	108.	Push-rod.
21.	Body.	65.	Spring—filler.	109.	Clevis pin—slave cylinder to clutch fork.
22.	Cover—body.	66.	Sealing ring.	110.	Washer—plain.
23.	Gasket—cover.	67.	Bolt—cylinder to brake plate ($\frac{5}{16}''$).	111.	Bolt—slave cylinder to gearbox.
24.	Screw—cover to body.	68.	Spring washer—cylinder bolt.	112.	Washer—spring.
25.	Washer—shakeproof.	69.	Bolt—cylinder to brake plate ($\frac{1}{4}''$).	113.	Bleeder screw.
26.	Spring—piston return.	70.	Spring washer—cylinder bolt.	114.	Banjo—slave cylinder.
27.	Retainer—spring.	71.	Screw—bleeder.	115.	Bolt—banjo—slave cylinder.
28.	Piston.	72.	Plate—L/H rear brake.	116.	Gasket—banjo.
29.	Cup—primary—piston.	73.	Bolt—brake back-plate.	117.	Gasket—banjo.
30.	Cup—secondary—piston.	74.	Nut—brake back-plate.	118.	Master cylinder box.
31.	Washer—primary clip to piston.	75.	Washer—spring—brake back-plate.	119.	Screw box—master cylinder.
32.	Boot—push-rod.	76.	Shoe—lined—brake.	120.	Nut.
33.	Gasket—boot fixing plate.	77.	Spring—shoe pull-off.	121.	Washer—plain.
34.	Plate—boot fixing.	78.	Spring—shoe steady.	123.	Support bracket—L/H master cylinder box.
35.	Screw—plate.	79.	Spring—shoe tension.	124.	Screw—bracket to topping plate.
36.	Washer—shakeproof.	80.	Abutment strip—brake-shoe.	125.	Washer—spring.
37.	Cap—filler.	81.	Nut—abutment strip.	126.	Base plate assembly.
38.	Seal.	82.	Washer—spring.	127.	Screw.
39.	Body—valve.	83.	Adjuster.	128.	Screw—box to bracket rear.
40.	Cup.	84.	Mask—adjuster.	129.	Nut.
41.	Washer.	85.	Body—with abutment strip.	130.	Screw—bracket to base plate.
42.	Push-rod.	86.	Piston—with dust cover.	131.	Nut—bracket to base screw.
43.	Nut—locking.	87.	Seal.	132.	Plain washer.
44.	Yoke—push-rod—to pedal.	88.	Piston—hydraulic.	133.	Gasket—adaptor.

Nomenclature of the parts of the hydraulic system.

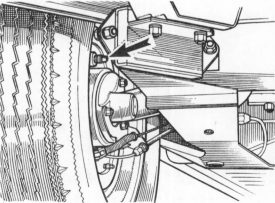

One square-headed adjusting screw is provided at each rear wheel brake.

The front wheel brakes have two such adjusters.

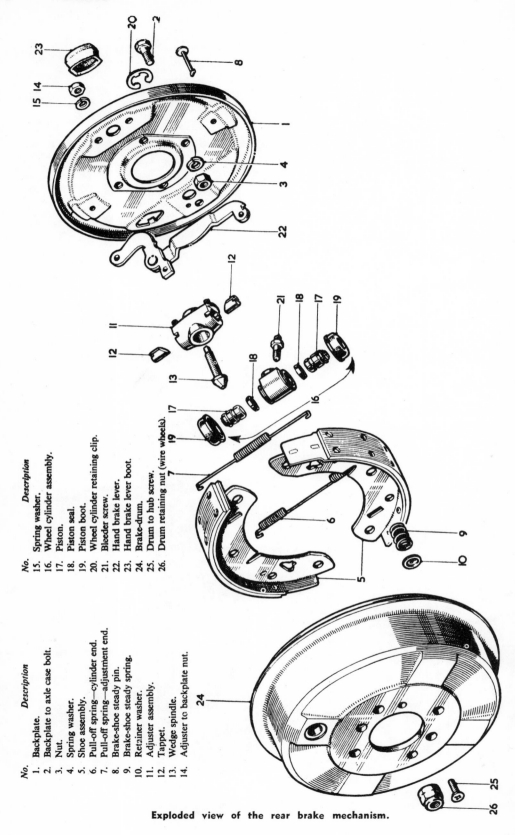

No.	Description
1.	Backplate.
2.	Backplate to axle case bolt.
3.	Nut.
4.	Spring washer.
5.	Shoe assembly.
6.	Pull-off spring—cylinder end.
7.	Pull-off spring—adjustment end.
8.	Brake-shoe steady pin.
9.	Brake-shoe steady spring.
10.	Retainer washer.
11.	Adjuster assembly.
12.	Tappet.
13.	Wedge spindle.
14.	Adjuster to backplate nut.

No.	Description
15.	Spring washer.
16.	Wheel cylinder assembly.
17.	Piston.
18.	Piston seal.
19.	Piston boot.
20.	Wheel cylinder retaining clip.
21.	Bleeder screw.
22.	Hand brake lever.
23.	Hand brake lever boot.
24.	Brake-drum.
25.	Drum to hub screw.
26.	Drum retaining nut (wire wheels).

Exploded view of the rear brake mechanism.

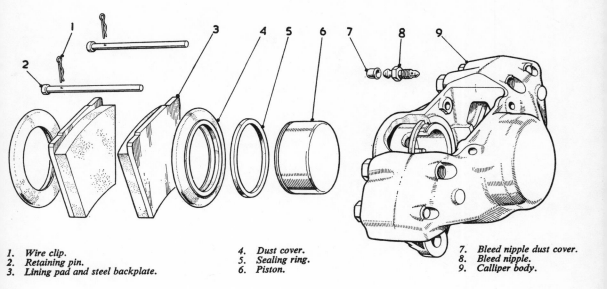

1. Wire clip.
2. Retaining pin.
3. Lining pad and steel backplate.

4. Dust cover.
5. Sealing ring.
6. Piston.

7. Bleed nipple dust cover.
8. Bleed nipple.
9. Calliper body.

Exploded view of the disc brakes used on the Austin-Healey and later Sprite models.

DISC BRAKE SERVICE PROCEDURES

RENEWING A SET OF FRICTION PADS

REMOVING. Jack up the car and remove the wheel. Depress the pad retaining spring and withdraw the cotter pins. Remove the spring and withdraw the friction pads using a rotational movement to assist. Because of limited space, it is necessary to remove the caliper from the disc and hub assembly on the MG-B models in order to renew the pads.

CLEANING AND INSPECTING. Clean the exposed face of each piston and the recess of each caliper to assure free movement. Press each piston back into the caliper. *CAUTION: While this is done, the fluid level of the master cylinder reservoir will rise, and surplus must be siphoned off to prevent its running over.*

INSTALLING THE PADS. Check that the relieved face of each piston is correctly positioned and install the new friction pad assemblies into the caliper. Install the anti-squeak shim between the piston and the friction pad. Make sure that the pad assemblies are free to move easily in the caliper recesses. Remove any high spots from the pad pressure plate by filing. Install the retaining spring, press down, and then insert the cotter pins. Operate the pedal several times to adjust the brake position. Add brake fluid as necessary.

BLEEDING THE BRAKES

Bleeding is required only when air gets into the lines. To remove the air, add brake fluid to the reservoir, attach a bleed tube to the bleed nipple, and immerse the free end of the tube in a clean jar containing some brake fluid. Open the bleed valve one turn, depress the brake pedal slowly, and then allow it to return slowly. Repeat until the fluid entering the jar is free of air bubbles.

PRESSURE REGULATING VALVE

A pressure regulating valve is installed in some models to prevent excess braking action on the rear wheels. In practice, the valve closes at a preset pressure, and all additional pressure is applied to the front wheel brakes. Service procedures consist of cleaning the unit and replacing the seals in the event of a leak.

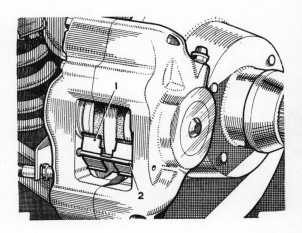

To remove the brake friction pads, depress the spring (1) and withdraw the pin (2).

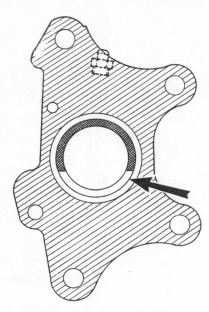

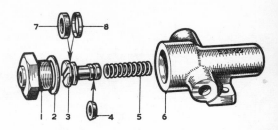

Details of the hydraulic pressure regulator used to limit rear wheel pressure on some of the lighter cars.

The cutaway part of the piston (arrow) must be assembled at the lower end of the caliper, opposite the bleed screw.